SALOONS
OF THE
AMERICAN WEST

Robert L. Brown

**AN ABANDONED SALOON in a Western ghost town—
the end of an era.** [Collection of Robert L. Brown]

DATE DUE

FEB 2 9 2008			
NOV 2 2009			
JUL 3 1 2008			
APR 1 0 2009			
SEP 0 1 2009			
NOV 2 5 2009			
JUL 3 0 2010			
JAN 1 9 2011			

SALOONS
OF THE
AMERICAN WEST

An Illustrated Chronicle

By

ROBERT L. BROWN

SALOONS
OF THE
AMERICAN WEST

An Illustrated Chronicle
By
ROBERT L. BROWN

For MADAM EVELYN

my wife and best friend for more
than three decades.

ROBERT L. BROWN

For many years, Robert L. Brown has been gathering detailed information and material for his books about the American West—including countless color transparencies. His efforts in this respect have taken him to literally hundreds of ghost towns and historic sites throughout the West.

Mr. Brown's teaching experiences include the University of Denver, the Denver Public Schools and the University of Colorado. His teaching areas are Western History and the History of Colorado.

He has written seven books to date, including his latest, "SALOONS OF THE AMERICAN WEST." Three are concerned with ghost towns and are titled "Jeep Trails to Colorado Ghost Towns," "Ghost Towns of the Colorado Rockies," and "Colorado Ghost Towns, Past and Present." "Holy Cross, the Mountain and the City" and "An Empire of Silver" are regional histories. "Uphill Both Ways" concerns Colorado's hiking trails and was published in 1976.

Mr. Brown holds memberships in the Colorado Authors League, Western Writers of America, and he served as Sheriff of the Denver Posse of the Westerners in 1969. In spare moments, he records talking books for the Colorado State Library for the Blind. Both Robert L. Brown and his wife, Evelyn, are active members of the Colorado Mountain Club.

Graphical Presentation —
   Sundance Publications, Ltd., Silverton, Colorado

Photolithography —
   Publishers Press, Salt Lake City, Utah

Binding —
   Mountain States Bindery, Salt Lake City, Utah

Editor-in-Chief — Russ Collman
Production Manager — Dell A. McCoy
Photo Director — John Shufelt

ISBN — 0-913582-24-7

First Printing — September, 1978

Foreword and Acknowlegments

Concerning the research and preparation of this book, the writer has incurred debts with a fairly extensive number of persons, sources and organizations, and gratitude should be expressed in all cases.

To begin, the original idea for this volume came from Mr. James Davis, formerly with the Denver Public Library's fine Western History Department. Jim Davis provided ideas, too; he helped with the organization of subject matter, ferreted out rare photographs and made many primary and secondary resource materials available. At this same source I was also assisted by Mrs. Opal Harber, Mrs. Hazel Lundberg, and by Mrs. Alys Freeze, director.

Additional materials and some photographs relating to this subject were found at the library of the State Historical Society of Colorado, where I was helped by Mrs. Enid Thompson and Mr. Terry Mangan. Dr. William H. Anderson Jr. of Denver took the time to recall memories of the years he spent in Nevada and Idaho concerning saloons at Reno and Boise, and in some of the surrounding towns. Louis Carter of Central City was of great help in supplying information about the saloons of Gilpin County, Colorado. Fred and the late Jo Mazzulla — fine historians and valued friends — produced both information and several unusual pictures from their vast collection. Other photographs came from the fine collection of Freda and Francis B. Rizzari. The Rizzaris also turned in their usual thorough job of reading and editing the completed manuscript, the seventh time they have performed this arduous and time-consuming task for me. A special word of gratitude also goes to Mrs. Jane Bass of Ft. Collins for reading the manuscript and for suggestions about the chapter on Bar Bottles.

Several additional photographs came from the superb collection of my good friend, Richard A. Ronzio of Golden. Jim Wright of Westminster, a long-time aficionado of saloon history supplied others. Mr. Wright, the late Dr. Philip Whiteley, and Mr. Sid Squibb of Central City were the sources of a great deal of the information in the chapter on saloon tokens. Other pictures came from Theron Fox of San Jose, California, and Miss Marion Williver of the Nevada State Historical Society. Charles Jones and Arthur Abe of Denver assisted with technical photographic problems.

Mary Valdez did much of the preliminary typing. My wife, Evelyn McCall Brown, typed the final revised manuscript and has helped in dozens of other ways with this project over the past several years. A separate bibliography lists the most valuable of the books, documents and manuscripts that were consulted.

For the chapter on saloon music I was assisted by Misses Norma Jean Lamb and Elaine Schutta of the Music Department, Buffalo, New York, and Erie County Public Library; Mrs. Bessie H. Smith, Music Librarian, Baylor University; and by the Music and Performing Arts Department of the Detroit Public Library. Some others made tapes for me and submitted to personal interviews.

One debatable but minor point: for the sake of consistency, the spelling, "whisky," has been used throughout, except for a few specific references and definite brand names. Historically, the word seems to have had no "e" in its original form. In a contemporary sense, "whisky" connotes Scotch and Canadian variations while "whiskey" refers to bourbon.

Likewise, since saloon etiquette, customs, practices and attitudes varied widely, and since the laws governing the operation of saloons were by no means uniform, the reader may find some accounts at variance with things you may have heard, seen, read or been told. Really, only the products sold and sometimes the personalities of bartenders were similar. In no instance have I knowingly presented events as facts without good authority, or have I intentionally colored what happened by my own literary style or ideas of what might have been. Whenever a "story" has been included, it has been labeled as such. For all such unresolved errors of interpretation, real or imagined, the writer apologizes in advance.

Finally, lacking the contributions of all of the previously listed persons, organizations and institutions, my task would have been infinitely more difficult, perhaps impossible. To all of them go my heartfelt thanks.

Robert L. Brown

TABLE OF CONTENTS

CRIPPLE CREEK'S FOUNTAIN SALOON was a popular watering place on notorious Myers Avenue. Note the separate wine room entrance—probably for ladies. [Cripple Creek Historical Society]

INTRODUCTION

Reduced to its most elementary terms, this book represents an effort to examine, with text and illustrations, some facets of the development of the American West in terms of the evolution of a singular institution — the *saloon*. Although the word now carries a rather negative connotation in present-day America, an enormous amount of United States history occurred in, or was influenced by, the saloon.

The general opinion in America regarding public drinking establishments became so fixed around the turn of the century that now only a handful of states, mostly in the West, still allow even the word "saloon" to be displayed on public signs, and much of its questionable reputation was deserved, as will become apparent in the unfolding chapters of this volume. Some of the very worst examples of human callousness toward others occurred beyond the swinging doors or in the alleys behind such places.

But now and then, acts of uncommon human kindness also took place within these rude establishments. Preachers were ordained, weddings and christenings were carried out, church services were performed and medical emergencies were taken care of, too — all within saloons. In common with nearly every other institution of a controversial nature, the saloon was neither all bad nor all good. There are definitely two sides to the story.

Inevitably, since Colorado is the author's home base, the saloons and history of this state have been used as examples more frequently than those of other states. Primary research sources are readily available here and can be cross-checked more easily. Generally, what happened in one state's saloons also happened elsewhere. The differences were not that great.

Today, however, such attractions as the mouth-watering free lunch, the technique of picking up a dime from a wet bar, and the sheer intellectual pleasure of discussing current events with the bartender are hardly more than fond memories for the small number of survivors who still recall the American saloon era.

In 1835, the 200,000 residents of New York City could choose to imbibe in any of the more than 700 saloons operating in the city at that time. Nearly 30 years later, when draft riots against the Civil War reached epidemic proportions, it was widely felt that most of the organized resistance to induction had originated in the 3,000 saloons that existed there by 1862. By 1884, Bowery saloons averaged a half dozen per block, and growth did not stop there. Some of the toughest dives, tucked away in side streets, were not family oriented, but were really places of violence. One such place in Memphis had its own private brand of whisky called "A Fight in Fifteen Minutes."

In the beginning, most labor unions opposed saloons, demanding Sunday closings in the hope of organizing bartenders.

Except for a few family towns like Gold Hill and Saints John, Colorado, where liquor outlets were rejected in open option elections, every town had at least one saloon. Men who considered themselves the bosses of their households could go to the saloon and lie about other things, too, on their weekly "night out with the boys." As the optimum symbol of male superiority, the saloon was likewise a refuge away from home in times of marital discord. Safely entrenched among his own peers in the local barroom, a man could gamble, hear popular tunes, drink, sit with his elbows on the table, spit on the sawdust floor, plunge into the free lunch, play cards, talk business, or just take it easy.

Saloons represented excitement of a sort and a variation from conventional pastimes in a rather lonely and unsettled period of U.S. history. They also offered a welcome change from the 12-hour work day. In some districts peopled heavily with first-generation immigrants, drinking was almost the only recreation of the poor. Exclusive clubs existed for the affluent, lodges flourished for the middle classes, leaving only the saloon for the poor. Intoxication helped to cushion the wretchedness of their pattern of life, and for some, it provided a brief escape from nagging wives and caterwauling children, caught up in different facets of the same syndrome that none of them understood.

But irrespective of one's station in life, the frustrations were there, and drinking was surprisingly common in early America. Not long after his departure from the White House, the late President Harry S. Truman gave a rather lengthy interview to a CBS newsman. At one point, the President digressed into a description of his first paying job. A local druggist in Independence, Missouri, had hired him to sweep the store, dust the merchandise, etc. Mr. Truman recalled that Independence had many saloons, but several of the leading citizens would not consider being seen in such places. So the druggist helped them out. Each morning a steady stream of businessmen visited the prescription counter. Each man placed a coin on the showcase, stepped behind the racks and helped himself to a heavy pull on a certain bottle.

So, whatever their concerns, lots of Americans spent off moments inside the thousands of drinking houses, and an occasional drugstore, which have flourished on these shores ever since those first boats from Europe deposited the initial clusters of colonists along our Atlantic seaboard. As the nation began to emerge and take shape, so did its various institutions, including saloons. With time, both the people and their traditions were modified through mutual cultural contact, assuming new roles while adopting different characteristics.

The first colonial American ale houses were as different from the West's frontier saloons as New York's prohibition speakeasies were from our modern co-ed bars. Only the brews that were dispensed bore any marked similarity. *Saloons of the American West* will recount this evolution, the good along with the bad, its side effects and its influence on U.S. history as Americans sought out differing solutions to life's vexations. And some of this was done within the framework of the changing but limited environment of the saloon.

Robert L. Brown

THE TINY JOE DENNY SALOON still stands beside the famous Cariboo Trail in the gold-rush town of Barkerville, British Columbia. Barkerville was primarily made up of American gold-seekers. [Collection of Robert L. Brown]

Chapter 1

IN THE BEGINNING —————————————————————————

ALMOST ASSUREDLY, the record of mankind's drinking habits antedates the dawn of recorded history. The discovery that the character of various grains and vegetables could be altered by fermentation is a very ancient bit of knowledge. Just when or by whom this was discovered remains nebulous. But in Genesis IX: 20, 21, we may read one of the earlier recorded references.

> And Noah began to be a husbandman, and he planted
> a vineyard; And he drank of the wine, and was drunk-
> en and he was uncovered within his tent.

Drinking was surprisingly common in 19th-Century America. Wine, spirits and fiery punches were both acceptable and expected on most dinner tables. A shortage of alcoholic drinks was almost an emergency. Like Louisville, Kentucky; Milwaukee, Wisconsin; or Golden, Colorado, towns often supported their local breweries with a sense of pride usually reserved for parks, churches or schools. In part, this may have been a carry-over from our European heritage, where local water supplies were unfit for human use. Saloons — by one name or another — have flourished in America for more than three centuries. There was even one at Jamestown, Virginia, in 1607.

Using molasses from the West Indies, rum-makers started about 1700. Other processes had been discovered much earlier. In 1730, John Adams said that, ". . . saloons make idlers, sots, thieves, and consumptive patients." He also noted that, ". . . you might as well preach to the Indians against rum as to our own people." The poor made beer out of molasses and bran, persimmons, potatoes, corn stalks, pumpkins or any other vegetables that could be made to ferment. In New England, the farmers made sassafras, spruce or birch beer, as well as hard cider.

Since drinking alone is not much fun, public drinking houses evolved. Here, men could meet to discuss all sorts of things. In many colonial towns, men gathered in saloons simply because these were the only places in which they could socialize with dirty hands and faces. Churches, club rooms, reading rooms and libraries would not permit dirt or rough talk, and most of their wives discouraged such practices at home. Nobody in a saloon told them to "go change your dirty clothes before you come to the table."

In colonial America, long before the westward movement began, the names "tavern" and "ordinary" were used to designate those places where one could buy liquor by the drink. Williamsburg, Virginia, our first colonial capitol, had many such places. Notable among them was Jean Marot's Ordinary, started in 1708. Marot was a French Huguenot who came over as a servant. Twice in his career he was indicted for selling liquor at rates higher than local laws permitted. In the same city, Burdette's Ordinary had billiard tables and sleeping rooms, but chiefly was used for drinking and gambling.

In Francis Sharp's Red Lion Inn, or Tavern, unlawful gaming was banned. He also boasted that

BECKER'S POOL ROOM was a favorite place for miners to relax in 1903 at Turret, Colorado. [State Historical Society of Colorado]

"on the Sabbath, no person shall be suffered to tipple or drink more than is necessary." The King's Arms Tavern boasted a particularly fine wine menu, plus the added attraction of a superb formal garden at the rear. Baron Von Steuben, the intensely partisan Prussian ally of General Washington, once ran up a bill of nearly 300 pounds for drinks and lodging at the King's Arms.

Best known of all the Williamsburg grog shops was the many-gabled Raleigh Tavern, where planters and businessmen gathered to exchange news. It was probably the greatest social center in town for the near-aristocracy. Washington often ate here, but stayed elsewhere because he considered the Raleigh too noisy. Gambling was popular — dice games in particular. Ale in pewter tankards, hot rum punches and Madeira wines were the specialties of the house. After an evening

at the Raleigh, a red-haired student at the College of William and Mary wrote, "I never could have thought the succeeding sun would have seen me so wretched as I now am!" His name was Thomas Jefferson. One author insists that the rebellious plotting for the American Revolution was done over the ale tankards at the Raleigh.

Josiah Chowning's Tavern still operates as an ale house in restored Williamsburg. Spicy punches, fine wines, ales and beer are served with oysters and thick slices of homemade French bread. Chowning's catered to a less august clientele than did the Raleigh or the King's Arms. Chowning's had no formal garden, but it did offer horseshoe pits within a yard at the rear.

Much of the pre-revolutionary oratory was a product of the Queen's Head Tavern at Broad and Pearl streets in New York City. General Clinton

THE HENRY FLEITER SALOON was located at 15th and Pearl streets in Boulder, Colorado. Note the mess around the spittoons. [Western History Collection—Denver Public Library]

hosted a great celebration of victory in this saloon after the colonial defeat of the British. George Washington attended as an honored guest. Thirteen toasts — one for each colony — were drunk. Ten days later, Washington bade his famed farewell to his staff in this same tavern.

In 1644, Connecticut passed a law forcing every community to open and maintain a tavern. Massachusetts' general court enacted a similar ordinance in 1656. When Newberry, Massachusetts, rebelled, it was fined twice in 1682 for not having a bar where travelers could "wet their whistles." Concord also was fined for the identical shortcoming. In some early New England towns, people were given free pasturage or exemptions from regular or church taxes if they would start a bar. Also in Massachusetts, people could be fined for drinking steadily for more than a hour. Common drunks got a variation on the Scarlet Letter routine: they were made to parade around the town with a large red "D" on their coats.

In colonial days, town officials selected those persons who could serve malt liquor to "ye olde public." County judges, or the Board of Selectmen in rural New England, chose persons of sober habits as those most likely to conduct an orderly house of entertainment. Hours of operation, gambling and loud singing were subjects of saloon legislation. Public peace and quiet were the objectives, not social control.

Glasses and steins shelved back of the bar were often numbered to connote their 6 to 18-ounce capacities. Without regard to size, a glass of beer sold for a nickel. For the big customer, 12-quart bottles with a take-home basket sold for a dollar.

The infusion of certain European minority groups of that time also influenced American drinking habits and appetites. Religious persecution and potato famines had brought hordes of German and Irish immigrants to America. Both groups were habitual drinkers who had never been exposed to the moral arguments of American clergymen and would-be prohibitionists.

In 1842, a Prussian named Wagner set up a Philadelphia brewery that produced the first Lager beer in America. His entire work crew was imported from Munich and their success soon drove other beers, porters and ales out of the area's thirst parlors.

Among immigrant minorities, only the Irish

AT HISTORIC TOMBSTONE, Arizona, one of the most famous saloons, the Crystal Palace, has been fully restored and is now open to the public. The inset shows the Crystal Palace in earlier days. [Collection of Robert L. Brown. Inset: Western History Collection, Denver Public Library]

posed a serious threat to the occupational dominance of German bartenders. Perhaps because they were rarely successful as brewers, the Irish threat never really became serious. Using the rye grains they had raised on their Monongahela

was Jimmy Hart of Boise, Idaho, who had worked in California's gold fields previously. He arrived in Idaho in 1861 and worked as a bartender in Oro Fino and Florence. His Irish wit was always popular and many of his pronouncements found their way into *The Idaho Statesman.*

Most Idaho saloons resembled the one at Van Wyck, called the Pioneer, which was run by Carter and Halter. A highly polished wooden bar, a brass foot rail, brass spittoons and wooden sand boxes were standard fixtures. Most customers missed the sand box as often as they hit it. The still evident spatters indicate that many chewers didn't even aim. Pool and card games were played. The lighting was provided by carbide lamps. One reason advanced for the popularity of Irish saloons was the generally rebellious character of the owners with regard to closing times, plus the fact that Irish policemen rarely bothered them.

In the trans-Mississippi West of 19th-Century America, saloons fulfilled a very real social need. Quite often, saloons were the first business ventures in frontier towns and they surpassed many other ventures both in quantity and success. Pioneers on the frontier sometimes spent as much time in saloons as they did in the mines or on horseback. In settlements peopled almost exclusively by lonely bachelors, saloons offered someone to talk with and a warm place in which to sit and relax among the heavy odors of tobacco smoke, sweaty clothing and whisky.

Saloons offered an emotional release from hard work and job tensions, as well as sympathy for the lonely frontiersman. They also afforded their patrons good male company, an art show, a chance to discourse on issues of the day, liquid refreshments, a free lunch — and sometimes feminine companionship of a sort.

The prevailing spirit of equality among all men was another widely recognized characteristic of the saloon. Rich or poor, well-attired or otherwise, the corner dram shop was a great social leveler.

Rye whisky was preferred in Eastern saloons, while bourbon was popular in the West and South.

Valley farms, Scotch-Irish immigrants made the first whisky on this side of the ocean. Later, this same group staged the 1794 Whisky Rebellion against the unpopular Naturalization Act. The revolt collapsed when an army of 1,600 men was sent against them.

Many Irish immigrants who were driven from their homes by potato shortages migrated westward to the mining camps. Some came with railroad-construction gangs, while others came with the army. Many chose to stay. One of these

A "SHORT BEER" CHECK of the type widely used in saloons. [Collection of Robert L. Brown]

AT BOULDER, COLORADO, W. H Callahan's Saloon and Pool Hall stood at 1207 Pearl Street. [Western History Collection—Denver Public Library]

HERE WAS IRISH Tim Looney's Saloon, a favorite place for silver miners at Montezuma, Colorado. [Western History Collection—Denver Public Library]

THIS WAS THE GAMBLING ROOM of the Pioneer
Saloon at Leadville, Colorado. [Western History Collec-
tion-Denver Public Library]

Both were believed to be effective in warding off
effeminacy.

While no single set of criteria would be either
adequate or accurate as a description of the
American saloon, there are some fairly safe
generalizations shared by a majority of these
public drinking places. The bar ran along the wall
of the room's longest dimension, usually on the left
side as one entered through the swinging doors.
Many of the best bars were made of dark hard-
wood. Some were ornately hand-carved from oak
or mahogany and sometimes walnut. For the
"tonier" places, such bars were fastened together
with wooden pegs rather than screws or nails.
Many had hand-rubbed finishes that grew more
lustrous with years of common use.

An intricately ornamented bar and back-bar
around the diamond-dust mirror showed richness
and was suggestive of quality. Behind the bar itself
and in back of the shelves of bottles, most saloons
sported a large plate-glass mirror. Around its
border, an assortment of motto cards exhorted the
customer about such delicate examples of saloon
comportment as not hurrying the bartender,
asking for credit or spitting on the floor. One said,
"If you spit on the floor at home, spit on the floor
here. We want you to feel at home."

A bank of slot machines (one-armed bandits)
could often be found in an out-of-the-way corner.
Much of the floor space was occupied by gambling
equipment. A firearm of some sort was kept out of
sight, but always within easy reach of the silent,

17

[Oil Painting by Jack Roberts]　　　　　　　　　　　　　[Neil Mincer Collection]

THE QUARTET

but observant, dealer. At the back of the building, or sometimes upstairs, were private card rooms, redolent with tobacco smoke and badly lighted, where cowboys, bullwhackers, miners, drifters and professional gamblers huddled around crowded tables. Two or three times each hour they called for and consumed shots of bar whisky. Fights were common.

Generally, a saloon had at least one back door and several side doors for the use of special customers, hasty escapes, occasional visits by ladies and for access to the cribs out behind the main structure. Adjacent to one of the rear exits was the "bull pen." This unique feature consisted of a high board fence. When things got rough in the saloon,

one or more bouncers would throw the more obstreperous customers into the enclosure, where they remained until sober. Rarely did a patron emerge from the bull pen with any money in his pockets.

Saloon floors were mostly of the puncheon type, heavily covered with sawdust to catch the drip, plus any gold dust that might fall from a miner's poke. Small boys were hired to pan out the gold from the sawdust once a week. Sawdust floated while the heavier gold sank to the bottom of the pan. The image of the heavily pomaded bartender is likewise no coincidence. By casually running his hand through his hair after pinching out gold dust, the average barman could recover a tidy sum by

THE CLIPPER SALOON was almost an annex of the railway depot in Buena Vista, Colorado, and catered mainly to railway men and travelers. [Collection of Richard A. Ronzio]

the simple expedient of a nightly shampoo.

The origins of swinging doors as a standard saloon fixture remain nebulous. Certainly the principle is a very old one. Thomas Jefferson installed weighted, delayed-action swinging doors between the sewing and dining rooms of his home at Monticello. On saloons, these doors provided easy access or egress for unsteady persons with fumbling, poorly coordinated hands. For sensitive persons passing on the boardwalk outside, swinging doors provided a discreet screening from activities going on inside. At the same time, the open areas above and below the doors allowed the alluring sights, sounds and odors to eminate as reminders to entice regular customers inside.

And a certain amount of whimsical 19thCentury humor concerned itself with the "thirst parlors" behind the swinging doors. One example will suffice. Allegedly, three boys were arguing and bragging about an assortment of paternal prowesses, such as, "My dad can lick your dad," etc. Whereupon little Johnny Jones put in his two-bits'

OBVERSE AND REVERSE SIDES of the tokens from the Gem Saloon and the C&F Bar in Tonopah, Nevada. [Collection of Robert L. Brown]

1 Bill Adams 2 Tony Herick 3 Sumner Whitney 4 Mike Tussel 5 Herman Otto

NOTE THE WONDERFUL ASSORTMENT of Western stereotypes gathered outside McKillip & Doyle's Grand View Saloon in Midway, Colorado, during 1899. This picture illustrates the role of the saloon as a social leveler. [Collection of Les Herman]

worth; "That's nothing, you guys," he intoned, "my dad is a magician. Every time he walks down Main Street, he turns into a saloon." Certainly this was not great humor, but with only minor variations, this old bromide has been around for at least two centuries and does reflect the prevailing public attitude of uneasy tolerance toward public drinking places.

[Collection of Fritz Klinke]

OPPOSITE, ABOVE and BELOW: This rare interior view shows the Henry Rothouser Saloon in Central City's Dostal Block during the 1890's. The bartender is August Bitzenhoffer. Note the oversize swinging doors. [Upper: Courtesy Gilpin County Historical Society.]

THIS EXTERIOR VIEW shows Whitney's Senate Saloon, a popular thirst quencher in the now-defunct town of Recen, Colorado. Recen was merged with Kokomo following a disastrous fire. [Collection of David S. Digerness]

THE ORIGINAL TIFFANY SALOON no longer stands at Cerrillos, New Mexico. It was destroyed in a fire during **1977.** [Collection of Robert L. Brown]

Chapter 2

WESTWARD HO!

AMERICA'S WESTWARD MIGRATION was not entirely composed of people who abused each other because of alcoholic excesses. Many were prudent, abstemious, family types — although we too often overlook such folks because writing of and reading about the others makes history so much more interesting.

To mention just one group, the Mormons, who settled in the Salt Lake Valley and south along the Mormon Corridor, did not use alcohol. In fact, all stimulants, including tobacco, coffee, tea — and today, even cola drinks — are theologically taboo. Saloons appeared in Mormon towns only after the California Gold Rush and the transcontinental railroad brought gentiles into their desert theocracy.

Even mining towns were known to have enforced saloon bans. An even greater number of towns founded on an agricultural basis also outlawed liquor vendors. Using Colorado as an example, Fort Collins, Boulder and Greeley all had anti-saloon planks in their original charters. None of the three remains a temperance community at present.

All of the experimental and somewhat classically socialistic farming communities founded by Horace Greeley and Nathan Meeker were dry towns. Greeley, an unusually fine man, was an ardent temperance crusader. When he visited the West to write stories about the gold discoveries for his *New York Tribune,* he usually made public speeches which invariably contained castigations of the "demon rum" and the saloonkeepers. At Central City, Colorado, the miners cheered one such speech lustily, but no evidence exists that they followed his advice.

Horace Greeley once wrote an opinion of the liquor served in the West. "I have not tasted it, but the smell I could not escape, and I am sure a more wholesome potable might be compounded of spirits of turpentine, *aqua fortis,* and steeped tobacco. Fully half of the earnings of our working men are fooled away on this abominable witch broth and its foster brother, tobacco." In earlier years, however, the situation was somewhat different.

American alcoholic appetites were legend. A remarkably large proportion of the lading bills included alcoholic beverages among the goods shipped across the Missouri River frontier. The socially accepted reason for this was that the booze was intended for medical uses. Many surviving diaries describe both the cargoes carried and the crudeness of trail saloons.

When people migrated westward along the Overland, Smoky Hill, Oregon, Santa Fe or other trails, the saloon went along as a cherished institution. During these migrations, there was a widely-held belief that whisky was an efficient, useful cure for rattlesnake bites. And so, according to tales told among temperance leaders in the East, many of the wagons that joined westbound caravans contained a case or two of whisky — and a box of snakes.

Like the ill-fated Donner Party, most westbound caravans adhered to a law of the plains concerning intoxication. Wagonmasters, guides and judges were appointed by and served at the pleasure of the group's members. It was one of the functions of a trail judge to enforce regulations concerning drunkenness. Commonly, the violator lost a day's pay. Repeated offenses caused him to be expelled on foot from the party with a canteen of water and five pounds of beef jerky.

One of America's earliest Far West saloons was set up in Browns Hole in the 1820's by Major Andrew Henry and General William Ashley, who had just bought out the St. Louis Missouri Fur Company. Their new venture was named the Rocky Mountain Fur Company. For almost two decades during the fur trade, Browns Hole was the largest settlement in the Rockies. Here, trappers, Indians and traders — about 5,000 of them — gathered for their annual rendezvous. Huge casks of whisky were packed out from St. Louis and sold directly from the keg. Raw corn-liquor and Taos Lightning were popular, too. Profits ran around 200 percent.

Trappers came in from their traplines after nearly a year of alcoholic drought and celibacy. The Indians brought squaws, and came to gamble and carouse. The result was a wilderness orgy every year through 1840, when fashion changes ruled out the popular beaver hat and the fur business collapsed. So did Browns Hole and its unique open-air saloon.

Westbound wagon trains, including those sponsored by the government, often set up informal tent saloons on the plains, on the deserts and in the mountains. And they held open house for all comers. One of the prairie thirst-quenchers was found on the Oregon Trail beside the Sweetwater River in present Wyoming. Underground ice formations were dug out of the earth at the famed Icy Slough, south of present Lander, and the wild mint that grew there enhanced the flavor of the intoxicants. This area is just east of the approach to historic South Pass.

Many enterprising emigrants loaded their Murphy, Conestoga or Studebaker wagons with oak barrels of wine, whisky, fiery punches or rum and set up improvised saloons along the way at convenient spots. Where the trails were rough or steep enough to induce work and, therefore, thirst, the barrel-top saloon could be expected on the top of the next hill. One example was seen beside the trail in the 1849 gold rush to California in Thousand Spring Valley near Elko, Nevada.

Dowell's saloon was another prairie watering place. It was fortuitously situated at El Paso, a point where the western extension of the Santa Fe Trail crossed the John Butterfield stagecoach route between San Antonio and the Pacific Coast. The Santa Fe Trail ceased to be an important route to the West on the day the high iron was extended from Lamy into the sleepy little adobe village of Santa Fe. However, Santa Fe was never an end-of-

24

THE LEADING SALOON of Black Hawk, Colorado, was called the Toll Gate because it was located at the terminus of the toll road from Golden. The Toll Gate offered other creature comforts, too. Note the saloon bawd seated in the upstairs window. [Collection of Richard A. Ronzio]

OBVERSE AND REVERSE of tokens from the Charles Lang Mirror Saloon, Glenwood Springs, Colorado, and the Horse Shoe Bar, Goldfield, Colorado. [Collection of Robert L. Brown]

tracks town. When workers arrived, they found that there were many saloons — some very old — waiting to serve them. One of the best was a mud-adobe structure with a huge bar, which was as long as the building. Three bilingual bartenders were on duty, and prepared to serve the railroaders Taos Lightning, Tequila or gringo popskull whisky.

But, down to the south, it was different. In 1706, a town called Albuquerque had been started. It grew when the Santa Fe Railway picked that spot for a division point. And, true to the traditional pattern, a Yankee saloon was in operation the first day, an open-air saloon with not even a brush lean-to or a tent for shelter. To avoid theft, the bartender dug a hole in the sand, hid his bottles and barrels in it, and laid boards across the top to make a floor for his barroom.

The West's earliest grog shops were housed in canvas tents. They consisted of little more than a few liquor barrels, supporting a rough-sawed board that functioned as the bar. Unwashed tin cups were used in the absence of the ornate glasses that appeared later. In Kansas, like other Western states, the first saloons were tents or dugouts by the trails, or shacks built from logs or rough boards. Barrels served as tables, and the bar consisted of a plank laid across two beer kegs.

One such primitive trail saloon, called the Bedrock, had log walls with crude shelves, a roof of pine boughs that sagged from the weight of the icicles and smoked hams that hung from its rafters. A barrel with a tin cup attached to a chain stood in the center of the room. Illumination consisted of tallow candles in miner's lights, stuck into the log walls. A huge fireplace at one end of the room helped light and heat the place.

Other types of tent saloons consisted of a large box with a wooden floor and three- or four-foot high walls. Two-by-fours, or whatever lumber was available, framed-in a skeleton roof. Heavy canvas was then stretched over the boards or, perhaps, between two trees and fastened to hooks or grommets on the outside walls. A few choice pieces of appropriate saloon art hung from the rough-hewn rafters. A crude frame door completed the structure. The whole thing could be collapsed rapidly for shipment on a wagon or railroad flatcar to a new location.

Usually a tent was used only until a log cabin could be erected. In the Southwest, the second home was probably of mud-adobe bricks. Still later, community prosperity probably dictated a move to a two-story structure of dressed lumber, supporting a fashionable false front. Quite commonly, the main building would be of notched log construction. But the front would be a false one, lending a sense of ersatz grandeur to status-conscious Westerners who lived in otherwise grubby surroundings. Saloon buildings at St. Elmo, Colorado, and at Nevada City and Virginia City, Montana, are of this type. In the more permanent camps, brick structures met with community favor. In fact, the status-conscious owner of the gin mill in Sopris, Colorado, called his place the Red Brick Saloon.

In pioneer days, because hard money was not plentiful, most purchases were made on the basis of barter. In one of the tent saloons located beside the Oregon Trail, a can of black powder could be swapped for a pint of whisky. Federal soldiers made the swaps both ways, depending on their needs of the moment.

When military expeditions met immigrant wagon trains on the Great Plains, a bar of some sort evolved as if by magic. There were many tent saloons along the better-known trails, and floating saloon barges and flatboats cruised the larger Western rivers. During construction days on the Kansas Pacific, Central Pacific, Union Pacific and other railroads, saloons and gambling halls were moved to the end-of-tracks locations along with the dance halls and dining tents.

When the Northern Pacific reached Forsythe,

OUR SPECIAL BRANDS.

KENWOOD.
SYCAMORE.
WELLINGTON.
GERMANIA CLUB.
GILT EDGE.

CABINET PURE RYE.

OLD CROW.
W.H. McBRAYER.
GUCKENHEIMER RYE.
FINCH'S RYE.

[Collection of Fritz Klinke]

THE CALIFORNIA BAR at Bingham Canyon, Utah, doubled as an Italian Boardinghouse for single men who worked in the copper mines. [Western History Collection—Denver Public Library]

OBVERSE AND REVERSE of tokens from the De Lamar Den Saloon, De Lamar, Idaho, and the Miners' Club Saloon, Ely, Nevada. [Collection of Robert L. Brown]

SPANISH ARCHITECTURAL INFLUENCE is evident in this saloon at Albuquerque, New Mexico. [Western History Collection—Denver Public Library]

Montana, 12 prefabricated saloons were unloaded in sections. Each was equipped with a regular bar, mirrors, tables with chairs, gaming equipment and the ever-present piano. Sometimes the glasses were being filled and the piano player was banging his instrument even before the roof had been laid.

As the frontier years passed, the colloquial term, "seeing the elephant," came to mean a seige of carousing and drinking in celebration of reaching trail's end or some similar purpose. But, originally,

the term had meant sighting California's coastal mountains, and hence, seeing the end of the trail — a rather obscure connotation. A popular trail song of that time was based on the same theme and told of crossing the pass to California. This folk melody may have been the source of the term, but there was no mention of drunkenness in the original libretto.

The earliest days in a new town were often both hectic and frustrating. Minot, North Dakota, had been in existence scarcely more than a month when it was found that there were already a dozen full-service saloons and a number of liquor-selling establishments that called themselves hotels. Conversely, there was only one church.

In some early frontier locations, the booze jugglers yielded to local temperance pressures by referring to their bars as "groceries." Pioneer writer, A. D. Richardson found a tent beside the trail north of Denver in 1859. It bore a grocery

OBVERSE AND REVERSE of tokens from the Condor Saloon, Anaconda, Montana, and the Mandolin Club Saloon, Globe, Arizona. [Collection of Robert L. Brown]

sign, but had no groceries inside; instead, it contained only two barrels of whisky, with a plank laid across them, while several unwashed tin cups sat in a row.

At the new town of Westport Landing, Kansas, James Ellis, a Missouri River whisky salesman, called a meeting in a local saloon that stood on high land above the Kaw River. After sampling the products of local brewers, the settlers abandoned the name of their settlement and adopted the name, Town of Kansas, as its new designation. Later, it became City of Kansas and, finally, Kansas City.

And so it went — Easterners became Westerners, establishing new towns and perpetuating many of their most cherished institutions. Such things as schools, churches and courts were transplanted from the East to the raw frontier, and one of the most-cherished institutions of all was the saloon.

THE RAWHIDE CLUB, tent-and-box combination, was the first saloon in Rawhide, Nevada. [Western History collection—Denver Public Library]

FREIGHT BILL.   D & R. G. Form 3741—10-00-200m   Silverton, Colo.   Station,   MAR 27 1901   190___

Antonio Giacomelli

To THE DENVER AND RIO GRANDE RAILROAD CO., Dr.

For Transportation and Advanced Charges, from_____ Via_____

BILLING REFERENCE.	DESCRIPTION OF ARTICLES.	WEIGHT.	RATE.	AMOUNT.
Pro. No. 775	2 bbl Whsky	700	170	11 90
W. B. No.	OR 30 gal			
Date of W. B. 3/26/01				
Car Initials.				
Car No.				
Consignor.	Advanced Charges. - -			11 34
(Give complete reference.)	Total.			23 24
				50
This form is the only authorized receipt to be given for payment of Freight Bills.	Received payment,_____ 190__			23 74
	W. M. M. _____ Agent.			

OBVERSE AND REVERSE of tokens from the Manhattan Saloon, Parma, Idaho, and the Mule's Ear Saloon. [Collection of Robert L. Brown]

THIS EARLY TENT-SALOON stood beside Willow Creek in Creede, Colorado, during 1892. [State Historical Society of Colorado]

AT BLACK HORSE, NEVADA, this 1907 tent saloon sported a fine array of saloon art. [Collection of Theron Fox]

[Collection of Fritz Klinke]

OPPOSITE, ABOVE: It seems as though the major recreation of Spar City in 1890 was playing cards and drinking spirituous beverages. Here, both are in progress in this print by an unknown photographer. [Collection of Richard A. Ronzio]

OPPOSITE, BELOW: The Louie Garbarina Saloon at 1100 Pearl Street in Boulder, Colorado, had no spittoons, and it sported a very messy floor. [Western History Collection—Denver Public Library]

Scene in Spar City, Colo.   Aug 1892

JARP

[Oil Painting by Jack Roberts]   **THE DANCERS**   [Ken Johnson Collection]

Chapter 3

SALOONS AND RECREATION ————————————————————————

WHILE ENGAGED IN RESEARCH for this chapter, the writer became convinced that the nature and scope of the diversions offered in public drinking places was limited only by the tolerance of the authorities and the imagination of the owner. While drinking remained as the primary attraction, there were many added inducements for visiting a saloon.

Games of chance of one sort or another probably outnumbered all other recreational forms. Saloon gambling games included keno, roulette, klondike, faro, blackjack and poker. Frequently the owner posted a female lookout in a chair atop a raised platform near the dealer. She watched the spread and helped to keep the dealer honest, at least where house profits were concerned.

Gambling and betting were popular saloon practices. Taking a chance on almost anything was a part of their way of life. Betting was common on anything that could move — such as pet turtles, rabbits and fleet-footed fire companies from rival towns. Wrestling matches and bare-knuckle boxing attracted big wagers. Sometimes a hungry promoter would raid the saloons looking for belligerent drunks, who would then be hired to settle their differences in the middle of the barroom. After missing swings in all directions, the antagonists then proceeded to give the most maladroit performance since the apocryphal antics of the topless lady accordionist.

Although saloon music is treated elsewhere in a separate chapter, it should be noted in passing that vocal and instrumental musicians were widely employed as a method of drawing street crowds inside. Frank Marryat, an English visitor in Sonora, California, described what he found in local saloons. "Drinking bars held forth inducements that nothing mortal is supposed to be able to resist. On a raised platform is a band of music, or perhaps Ethiopian serenaders; or, if a Mexican

saloon, a quartet of guitars; or in one house is a piano, and a lady in black velvet who sings in Italian and accompanies herself, and who elicits great admiration and applause on account of the scarcity of the fair sex. . . ."

Even the most vigorous of the spectator sports could be found in the bigger saloons. Among them were bullfights, cock fights and dog fights. Boxing exhibitions ended only when one man was beaten into insensibility. One match in 1865 in Virginia City, Montana began at 8:00 p.m. and ended in a draw at dawn after 185 rounds. The bar receipts remain unknown.

A count made in 1876 listed an even hundred saloons in Virginia City, Nevada. One of them was run by a 190-pound "ball of fire" named Madame Bulldog, the only woman who ever threw Calamity Jane Canary out of a thirst parlor. As Sunday entertainment, another saloon offered fights between bulldogs and wildcats. Several of the 30 saloons at Columbia, California, offered bull-and-bear fights as entertainment.

In pioneer Miles City, Montana, the wildest of the watering places were named the Gray Mule and Cosmopolitan. Both were saloons and both sported small theatres. Shapely bar girls were always in attendance. Patrons had to pass through the saloon to get to the theatre. It was planned that way, like today's food stores that place staples in the back, necessitating a tempting walk past all of the high-profit impulse items. The psychology of this arrangement is very old and was not unknown

LEADVILLE'S NOTORIOUS STATE STREET included the Theater Comique—shown at left. [State Historical Society of Colorado]

to saloonkeepers. By the same token, the gaming tables were located so as to make patrons stroll past the ever-present bar, reeking of aromatic suggestions. Likewise, the "cribs" of the girls, if any, were at the backs of the saloons, or on the second floor, and they were accessible only through the bar, of course.

Among first-generation Irish and German immigrants, bars and brothels sometimes were combined in the same establishment, often run by a husband and wife. The husband tended bar and his wife acted as the madam. Dr. William Sanger, sociological researcher, reported a four-year life span for prostitutes after entering this career—a statistic probably dictated more by crusading zeal and compassion than by actual facts.

Since family-type women in the West were in short supply, pioneers manifested a kind of amiable gallantry toward local *nymphs du prairie*. A common technique of these Western saloon girls

was to approach the customer and attempt to kick his hat off — a friendly thing to do and one sure to provoke conversation and to suggest obvious kinds of recreational experiences, plus a few ancillary services as well.

Mormons in Ogden, Utah, stayed far away from the gentile-owned Chapman Bar. They were particularly offended when — after Brigham Young's death — Gentile Kate's Toney Bagnio purchased Young's monogrammed coach. It was used to transport disreputable women around the Chapman Bar's neighborhood for "house calls."

The name "Hurdy-Gurdy Girl," like "Seeing the Elephant," was a misnomer. Hurdy-gurdies were street pianos, played by turning a crank. They were widely used by Eastern street musicians of Italian extraction, who kept an attention-getting monkey on a chain. After each soulful rendition, the monkey passed the tin cup among the street crowd.

THIS VIEW features a saloon and gambling den in one of the San Juan mining camps. [Western History Collection —Denver Public Library]

Saloons that were called hurdy-gurdies combined the salient features of a bar and a dime-a-dance hall, but there was no gambling. Some did not collect a dance fee, but dancers were expected to buy themselves and the "lady" a drink after each rat race around the floor. His drink cost a dollar and usually was "red eye" whisky. Hers cost the same, but was apt to be cold coffee or tea; and in a lonely frontier society, where women were either a rarity or a bargain, the hurdy-gurdy was a financial success with a 95-cent profit per dance. In some hurdy-gurdies you bought a metal token before the dance and redeemed it at the bar for drinks later, thus assuring a minimum of cheating on the house.

Many hurdy-gurdy girls were from Europe and had been "imported" by a man called the "boss hurdy," who bound them as indentured servants (illegally) until he felt that he had regained the cost of their transportation to the United States. Few of them could speak English, but they soon acquired

a vocabulary of the popular vulgarisms which they used indiscriminately for all occasions. The Barry & Adler Saloon at Barkerville, British Columbia, employed eight German hurdy-gurdy girls. The fire that nearly destroyed Barkerville in 1868 was started accidentally by one of these girls in the rooms above the saloon while she was pressing a dress.

Saloon women sometimes were forced into service as entertainers who danced, sang or told fortunes. Cripple Creek's Cabinet Saloon employed a fortune teller, Madame Vida De Vere, complete with crystal ball. It was popular to believe that she could locate mines. And, as a curiosity, she did manage to entice a lot of thirsty miners to the Cabinet's mahogany bar.

In some of the fancier saloons — sometimes called variety theatres — there were stages at the end of the room. Regular traveling shows were booked for nightly performances. On Leadville's notorious Chestnut Street, the Key Stone Saloon

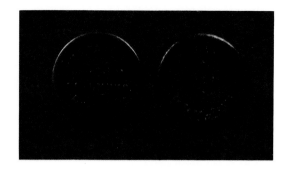

OBVERSE AND REVERSE of tokens from the Atlas Saloon, Columbus, Montana, and the Farmers' Exchange Saloon, La Jara, Colorado. [Collection of Robert L. Brown]

advertised a specialty act in which a man shot apples off the top of his wife's head with a Remington rifle. Variety theatres were only slightly more respectable than dancehalls. They combined the more salient features of saloons and burlesque houses.

In 1879, Leadville's Theater Comique, on notorious State Street, was rented for $1,700 a month. Since estimated daily receipts were about $1,200, this modest rectangular wooden structure always made money. Its "shows" started at 9:00 p.m. and ran until 2:00 a.m. Trouble came when balcony customers threw food and dropped liquor bottles down onto the audience on the main floor. Eddie Foy came to Leadville from Dodge City and performed at the Theater Comique in 1878. He recalled later having slept on a straw mat spread out on the stage. Rose Howland, a Leadville concert singer, became Mrs. Foy.

All-night saloons offered variety shows that

A FOURTH OF JULY scene at Meeker, Colorado, included the Rector & Davis Saloon. [State Historical Society of Colorado]

THE BUSY ORIENT SALOON at Bisbee, Arizona, looked like this in 1903. [Western History Collection—Denver Public Library]

OBVERSE AND REVERSE of tokens from the Whitacre & Crites Saloon, Fort Collins, Colorado, and the Spitzner Brothers Saloon, Silver Cliff, Colorado. [Collection of Robert L. Brown]

began at 8:00 p.m. and dropped the final curtain at 4:00 in the morning. Many of the performers were talented artists from Europe or the East. Profits from liquor were high enough to cover expenses and no admissions were charged. Saloon girls passed constantly among the tables, serving drinks to the all-male audience. Champagne cost $15 a bottle. At Dawson City in the Klondike, the price was $25 and boiled eggs sold for $2 each.

The classic tableau was used by some of the upper-class bistros as entertainment attractions. In one place, Neptune rose from the sea and Andromeda was seen chained to her rock. In another, scantily-clad female "Christian martyrs" did battle with ersatz lions, while tipsy audiences roared their approval. And when liquid refreshments were mixed with theatre, it sometimes became difficult to distinguish actors from spectators as the act spread into the audience. For example, one night in Tombstone, the "Paradise of Devils," Calamity Jane attended a show in a local saloon. As glass after glass passed her lips, she forgot that the villain was only an actor and took a shot at him. Fortunately, her alcoholic aim was bad and the actor was unscathed.

Sometimes an unusual claim to fame was used in conjunction with some theatrical feature to pack the place. At Erickson's in Portland, Oregon, the bar measured 684 linear feet. Erickson's also sported an all-girl orchestra. An electrically charged metal rail kept overly zealous admirers at arms length.

Since 19th-Century America equated size with quality, some of the saloons were enormous. In Columbia, California, the Long Tom extended from Main Street to Broadway and a pair of armed guards stood at each of its doors. Tex Rickard's Northern Saloon in Goldfield saw $7-million pass his cashier in two years. Twelve bartenders tended the 60-foot-long bar, claimed to have been the world's longest.

Saloons were sometimes regarded as status symbols. In common with certain churches that came to be preferred by one group or another as "the place" in which to be seen, some of the more elegant grog shops took on a special atmosphere. As a town acquired culture, certain saloons became "the watering place," and the most elite boozers would not countenance being found in another.

Treating — always encouraged by the bartender — became an important tradition of saloon etiquette and became synonomous with good fellowship. Good manners dictated that each gentleman should buy a round of drinks until all were "three sheets to the wind." High-school graduations, the

AN INTERIOR VIEW of the Sam Peterson Saloon in Kremmling, Colorado, is shown in this illustration. Note the

**presence of an under-aged boy at the left of the gambling
tables.** [Collection of Jim Andrews]

freedom of Ireland, new babies, Bastille Day, or Carry Nation's birthday were considered appropriate excuses for "setting them up for the crowd." Community traditions were always honored in saloons; holidays and anniversaries were observed; and the dead, especially Colonel Custer, were euologized in song, and especially in poetry. Both Robert Burns and Edgar Allen Poe were favorites of barroom poets. And in the present century, the works of Robert W. Service, which sometimes featured barrooms, were rendered with some frequency and much feeling.

Throwing away the key was a common practice when a new saloon had its grand opening. The doors, it boasted, would never again be closed, day or night. When a new saloon opened its doors for the first time in a town, a fun-filled celebration was likely to follow. A parade was expected. Clydesdale horses pulled gaily decorated beer wagons, while one or more German brass bands tootled the message of Old Heidelberg in three-quarter time. The mayor, city council, local potato-festival queens, small boys on decorated bicycles, and an array of canine pulchritude would also be in the order of march. In Western towns, the dancehall girls often rode in a coach near the end of the parade, ever alert to the chances for a bit of free advertising.

When the ribbon was cut and the thirsty crowd could enter the new saloon, brewers' representatives were on hand to dispense free samples. At the opening of the Monte Carlo Saloon in Dawson City, Alaska, the first patrons inside were greeted by a pretty dance-hall lassie who sat astride each barrel of spirits.

Special holidays were a mixed blessing for the liquor dispensers. Although extra time off work meant extra business for the thirst quenchers, there were problems, too. With a few drinks under their belts, drunken orators chose to hold forth for captive audiences in saloons, exhorting sinners to repent and extolling the virtues of Bastille Day, the Fourth of July, etc., and Salvation Army lassies with drum and bugle passed the tambourine among tipsy free-spending customers.

Riding a horse into a barroom was a common Western recreation. Colorado's Cripple Creek had several such instances. At the grand opening of the National Hotel's saloon at Fourth Street and Bennett Avenue, Spencer Penrose and a parlor-house girl rode horses up to the bar and ordered drinks. Cowboy Bob Womack rode his horse up the stairs of Colorado City's first parlor house, galloped across to the bar and demanded that the horse be served a beer. Stunts of this variety caused people to be dubious — so when Womack,

THIS INTERIOR VIEW shows another of the restored saloons at Barkerville, British Columbia. [Collection of Robert L. Brown]

AN INTERIOR VIEW of a saloon in Colorado's Central City. [Western History Collection—Denver Public Library]

OPPOSITE, ABOVE and BELOW: The William Stephens Saloon stood at the now-extinct town of Freeland, Colorado. Note the presence of at least two black men. The exterior scene shows the Sam Peterson Saloon at Kremmling, Colorado. [Above: Collection of Jim Wright. Below: Collection of Jim Andrews]

Durango, Co. Sept 23 1891

Moris Gicomelli

Silverton Colo

Bought of

J. KELLENBERGER,

DURANGO, COL. & 229 KINZIE ST. CHICAGO, ILL.

Wholesale Dealer & Importer of

WHISKIES, BRANDIES WINES & CIGARS.

& Sole Controller of the

FAMOUS COLUMBINE BRAND

OF

WHISKIES & CIGARS.

OBVERSE AND REVERSE of tokens from Turner Hall, Denver, and the Palace Hotel Bar, Cripple Creek, Colorado. [Collection of Robert L. Brown]

the town character, claimed to have found gold in the crater of an extinct volcano, it was only natural that he was disbelieved. But the gold was really there, and the result was fabulous Cripple Creek, the world's second-richest gold camp. But poor Bob Womack did not share in the riches. He got drunk in a local saloon to celebrate, sold his claim for $500 and died in poverty.

In a few saloons, surprisingly, the chief form of recreation was just plain drinking. The previously mentioned Erickson's Saloon occupied most of a city block on Burnside Street in Portland, Oregon. It lasted almost 40 years. It was founded in the 1880's by August Erickson and the interior featured five long bars that ran continuously around and across one huge room. A $5,000 pipe organ dispensed culture. Beers cost a nickel. Ladies could drink at Erickson's, but only in small

OLD SALOON with false front, boardwalk and hitching rail at Virginia City, Montana. [Collection of Robert L. Brown]

AT DIFFERENT TIMES, both William Stephens and F. M. Bertoldi operated this saloon in Freeland, Colorado. [Collection of Jim Wright]

OBVERSE AND REVERSE of tokens from the Colombo Saloon, Kellogg, Idaho, and the Big Casino, Tonopah, Nevada. [Collection of Robert L. Brown]

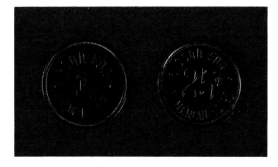

booths that lined the walls. In general, women were banned from Erickson's, except for that all-girl orchestra.

One logger told Gus Erickson, "When I want a woman, I know where to go. When I want a drink, I come here, and I don't see no sense mixing them together." Gus Erickson died in 1925 and his building has since been razed.

Erickson's traditional saloon art included the usual array of classic nudes, plus a huge painting called "The Slave Market." The free lunch included a roast quarter of beef and one and one-half-inch-thick slices of Swedish hardtack bread. The mustard pots held a quart. Erickson's bartenders were huge men who sported carefully tended mustaches, plastered-down hair, white vests and aprons, as well as oversize watch chains. White shirts with arm elastics completed the uniform.

THE OURAY SALOON, a popular "watering place" in upper Creede, Colorado, is shown at far right in this view. [State Historical Society of Colorado.]

Before the arrival of women, frontiersmen sometimes gathered at the saloon for an all-male dance. After partaking of liquid refreshments, the fiddler or piano player would take his place at the side of the room. Usually the men acting the part of ladies tied a bandana around one arm. Often they kicked their feet and swung their partners until dawn.

A Scotsman, J. D. Borthwick, described how racial discrimination worked in 1857 in California saloons. "Negroes were permitted to lose their money in the gambling rooms; and in the less-frequented drinking shops they might be seen receiving drinks. When a negro wanted accommodation, he waited until others had finished and had left the table before he ventured to sit down."

With prosperity, the saloons became more imposing. Maple tables and chairs, kerosene chandeliers, and oak or mahogany bars became common. Huge mirrors hung behind the shelves of spirits. Saloon mirrors were not merely ornamental; they were sometimes a means of protecting the customer from being shot in the back. In the plush saloons there might be carpeting rather than sawdust on the floors. When the rugs got a weekly cleaning, the recovered gold dust amounted to a tidy profit. Plush red-velvet curtains often covered the windows, and ornate chandeliers of red, green or blue glass hung from the ceiling and held large oil lamps. Most had an assortment of glass bangles

A STRANGE COMBINATION business, Spalti's Saloon and Bakery at 17th and Blake streets in Denver. [State Historical Society of Colorado]

of various shapes and sizes that hung from the brass frame of the fixture. Some of the fancier booze jugglers hired small boys who remained out of sight while squirting perfume into the air from upstairs balconies.

In the timber country of western Washington, lumberjacks often quenched their thirst at Big Fred Hewlett's Humboldt Saloon. It operated until 1920 in the town of Aberdeen. No woman of virtue, nor of any other persuasion, was allowed inside. Gamblers and card artists were likewise excluded in line with Hewlett's reputation for honesty. But there were other attractions. A huge array of mineral specimens from far-away places was on exhibit. Indian artifacts, a coin collection, freaks of nature in bottles of alcohol and stuffed animals completed the "educational" exhibit. So popular was the Humboldt that an entire new hemlock floor had to be installed twice each year — after Christmas and the Fourth of July.

However, saloon recreation still survives. At Cripple Creek's Imperial Hotel, a melodrama plays two shows a day to packed houses in its barroom theatre during the summer months. And at Cerrillos, New Mexico, Pat Hogan's Saloon and the Graham Brother's Cantina had swinging doors that rarely stopped. Tiffany's Saloon, also in Cerrillos, has been in operation since 1860. Spittoons are hand-polished. Its barroom is 100 x 50 feet. Some of the original bar has survived, complete with bullet holes. The mirrors have been replaced many times. Animal heads decorate the walls beside old posters. It now has summer-evening melodrama performances, too.

The same degree of social deprivation that resulted in the saloon becoming almost the only place where one could meet friends or engage in camaraderie of any sort, also dictated the common means of passing the time for families and non-saloon people. For most, hymn singing and

OBVERSE AND REVERSE of tokens from the Reiterer Vienna Saloon, Sopris, Colorado, and the Schaydt Brothers Saloon. [Collection of Robert L. Brown]

story telling were common pastimes. And at times, the latter activity also found its way through the swinging doors. At Austin, Nevada, there were regular meetings of a loosely drawn group of lonely males known as the Sazerac Lying Club. Harmless fabrications of the truth dominated their gatherings and filled their idle hours. Needless to say, they met in an Austin saloon. A false-fronted building bearing the Sazerac Saloon name still stands in Virginia City, Nevada.

Fred Hart, a relative of Brett, was one of the organizers of the Sazerac Lying Club. Hart, like Mark Twain, was employed by *The Territorial Enterprise*. The club's first rule insisted that all lies must be true. Hart published a book in 1878 called the *Sazerac Lying Club*. It was printed in San Francisco and was mainly an anthology of the tall tales told at the saloon.

Like other seasonal business ventures, the bar business was also affected by the weather and the time of year. Notable increases in saloon visitations occurred with the arrival of the first chill blasts of winter. Activities like bowling, gambling and shuffleboard were moved indoors and combined with liquid refreshments, and another season of saloon-centered recreation was off to a roaring start.

WOODEN BEER KEGS were stored along the wall at the Andy Nelson Saloon, 1400 Pearl Street, Boulder, Colorado. Evidence of poor aim can be seen on the floor beside the spittoons. [Western History Collection— Denver Public Library]

OPPOSITE, BELOW: Cripple Creek, Colorado, was the scene of this saloon picture. Note the poor marksmanship spots around the spittoons. [Western History Collection— Denver Public Library]

OBVERSE AND REVERSE of tokens from the Haden Saloon and the Farmers' Exchange Saloon, La Jara, Colorado. [Collection of Robert L. Brown]

THIS RARE PICTURE shows the free-lunch table in one of the Sam Peterson saloons. Bar towels which had been hung on the bar front allowed customers to wipe the suds from their mustaches. [Collection of Jim Andrews]

HERE IS AN EXAMPLE of barroom art from the Grand Imperial Hotel in Silverton, Colorado. [Photo by Dell A. McCoy]

Chapter 4
SALOON ART

SALOON DECORATIONS — except for the huge, ornate chandeliers and mirrors — reflected unmistakable male tastes. Even the saloon names suggested masculinity. A few were named for the proprietor, but most bore designations like Last Chance, Miner's Exchange, Pastime, Smoke House, Mule's Ear, Bucket of Blood, Longhorn, Gold Nugget, Casino, Miner's Delight, or Bull's Head. But there were exceptions, too, like Patty Carrol's in Silverton, The Daisy at Leadville, or the Blue Bird Saloon at Moffat — all in Colorado.

Many brewers supplied colored ads that lent a festive touch to drab saloon walls. In San Antonio, the Buckhorn Saloon was adorned with a collection of hunting trophies that included deer-and-elk antlers, mounted snake skins, steer horns and a caged macaw parrot near the front doors. Those who entered were greeted with profane proclamations or allusions concerning their ancestry as they passed the cage.

In the 1890's, more than 50,000 photographs of John L. Sullivan were distributed for display in saloons. The bibulous champion was a favorite of bartenders since he made a practice of entering saloons frequently and "setting them up" for all present.

Other forms of saloon art that were popular at the time included temperance pledge cards, bought up for the price of a few free drinks. The cards were slipped into the edges of mirror frames and displayed as proper trophies. Witty signs and snappy sayings were tacked up in every open space. Some of the larger ones, printed to resemble "Home Sweet Home" samplers, were framed and hung about the walls. Examples of these old bromides included such homilies as "Don't forget to write to Mother; we furnish free paper and envelopes," "We serve the best wines and liquors in town," "If drinking interferes with your business, cut out the business," or "Grandma, throw down your corset, we need a hammock in the backyard."

The unfinished portrait of George Washington by Gilbert Stuart was one of the most universally displayed 19th-Century paintings that adorned saloon walls. Seafaring paintings, whaling expeditions and depictions of heroic and patriotic scenes were likewise popular. Steel engravings of our first 15 or so presidents were often displayed in barrooms. And back in a dark corner, one would likely find a popular photograph that had been distributed by the thousands from a Louisville distiller in the 1880's. It showed an Indian baby nursing at his mother's breast. Below the photo was a caption, "Hot Meals Served at All Hours." Some tasteless saloonists displayed this inappropriate poster above the free-lunch counter.

But there was one art form that probably outnumbered all of the other attempts at cultural uplift combined. Quite naturally, this was the female figure, preferably undraped, and the bigger the better. Most saloon art depicted a somewhat-pudgy feminine form, shaped like a bass violin, the almost entirely circumferential specimens so idealized by Victorian males. An alluring expanse of beefy leg was always in evidence. Outright pornography was rarely seen. Suggestion was the thing that drove grown men mad! *September Morn, Diana in the Bath* and *Venus Surprised* were exhibited frequently.

Nevertheless, a few saloons did go in for shameless pornography. While "bar-hopping" in San Francisco, Hinton R. Helper saw ". . . the walls of

PRIOR TO THE CURRENT RESTORATIONS, this was Central City's famous Teller House Bar. Note the classic types of saloon art. [State Historical Society of Colorado]

OPPOSITE, ABOVE and BELOW: This saloon in Telluride, Colorado, sported quite a display of barroom art, gambling equipment and the local sheriff. [Western History Collection —Denver Public Library]

The scene below was in the Turf Exchange Saloon in Como, Colorado, a favorite spot with railroaders after the South Park Line reached there in 1879. The wall decor suggests that the saloonkeeper must have been a horse fancier and liked harness racing. [Collection of David S. Digerness]

a certain saloon where all available space was covered with paintings and engravings of nude women in every imaginable posture of obscenity and indecency."

New York's tasteful Hoffman House was a widely known bar for the city's wealthy playboys. Its nude paintings were bigger and more revealing. The classic *Nymphs and Satyr* hung on the wall opposite a huge bar, a very sophisticated piece of saloon art. Other famous saloon paintings included *The Ballet Dancer* and *The Wedding at Cana in Galilee.*

In nearly all saloons, the greatest attraction was the larger-than-life painting of a heroically endowed reclining lady. Due to room proportions, horizontal compositions were preferred. Most depicted a well-endowed young girl whose posture suggested her readiness to take either a nap or a bath. The preferred positioning for saloon art was

CUSTER'S LAST FIGHT was one of the most used examples of saloon art in America. This version hangs in the Grand Imperial Hotel, Silverton, Colorado. [Photo by Dell A. McCoy]

barely above the eye level of the men standing at the bar. Owners sometimes made pocket money from their less-observant friends by betting that no customer would drink at the bar within a specified time interval without at least one furtive glance at the barroom art display. Fancier "joints," with more available wall space, displayed not just one, but several of these nubile nymphs.

Of course, not all saloon art was devoted to the undraped female form. Many paintings portrayed heroic scenes from history, nostalgic interludes or great lost causes. One of the most widely used of all was a huge canvas of the Custer debacle of June 25, 1876.

Sometime in the 1890's, the Anheuser-Busch Company redeemed the mortgage of a St. Louis saloon at Eighth and Olive streets that had defaulted on $10,000 of its payments. When the physical assets of the business were inventoried, company representatives found an enormous canvas titled "Custer's Last Stand." Artist Cassilly Adams had executed the work sometime in the 1880's for use in a cyclorama with a traveling carnival, but the show folded. Adams had hired a few Sioux to pose for him in his studio to be sure

HANSEN'S SALOON in Genoa, Nevada. Notice the display of saloon art behind the bar. [Nevada State Historical Society]

of an authentic depiction. Attempts to sell the work in St. Louis art stores met with failure. Adams stored the work in the saloon, but probably did not sell it to the proprietor. Nevertheless, at least 2,000 lithographic copies of the Adams canvas were distributed by Anheuser-Busch to saloons that used their product.

By no means the worst of the many artistic efforts to depict the demise of Custer, the painting perpetuated at least three serious errors. First of all, it showed Custer standing on the hill, although most students of the fight, including the Sioux, insist he was shot from his horse at the river and that his body was carried back up onto the hill by the retreating troopers. Second, it showed Colonel Custer with long hair. It was a hot summer, and most of the 7th Cavalry — including Custer — had

been shorn of their locks at Fort Abraham Lincoln. Finally, the saber in Custer's hand constituted more artistic license. These clanking, noisy weapons were left aboard the steamboat, *Far West*, simply because they would have betrayed the troops' presence to alert Sioux ears. But the picture's background was flawless — the troop positions being essentially correct and Custer properly shown in buckskin attire. Anyway, it was a heroic example of great saloon art and it met with enormous approval.

Predictably, the men of the 7th Cavalry wanted the original canvas, and Anheuser-Busch presented it in "dry" Kansas, at Fort Riley. In keeping with the occasion, the company presented the 7th with enough of their brew to float the entire Little Bighorn battlefield. Later, the painting went to

THE WINCHESTER SALOON in Rifle, Colorado, obviously believed in a patriotic display along with its saloon art. [State Historical Society of Colorado]

Fort Grant, Arizona, where somebody "misplaced" it. Then it reappeared mysteriously at Fort Bliss, Texas, in the Officer's Club, of course. It was destroyed when the building burned down in June of 1946.

A second artist named Becker copied the Adams canvas for the brewery. Both paintings are alike, except for one detail. For some unknown reason, Becker had Custer waving a sword above his head. In the original Adams version, he was stabbing a Sioux with it. Both artists erred by placing the weapon in Custer's right hand. George Custer was left-handed. A surprising number of the multi-colored lithographs that survived, including the one reproduced in this book, bear the signature O. Becker. The Adams versions are much rarer.

Perhaps the most famous drinking argument in history is the one that raged in American saloons for nearly three-quarters of a century. It seems unlikely in this sophisticated era, but men actually fought each other with fists and knives — and there were a few shootings, too. The basic dispute concerns whether Custer and his troops were drunk the night before their final battle. Many Indians, anxious to discredit "Yellow Hair," claim that they were. News of the alcoholic orgy, duly reported by Sioux scouts, was the thing that allegedly caused Two Moons, Gall and the medicine man, Sitting Bull, to stand and fight that day.

OVERLEAF, ON PAGES 62 and 63: The painting portrayed on Page 62 is a typical barroom nude and once adorned a saloon in Telluride, Colorado. The subject was a popular "girl of the line." The handsome saloon canvas reproduced on Page 63 hangs in the restored barroom of the South Park City museum display in Fairplay, Colorado. [Collection of Robert L. Brown]

FRITZ THOME'S Rio Grande Saloon in Cripple Creek is portrayed in this exterior view. Note the "free lunch" invitation on the door. [Western History Collection—Denver Public Library]

The opposing viewpoint holds that the 7th was cold-sober and fell into a trap. One Montana saloon customer, too long in his cups, publicly expressed the theory that "Custer was drunk" one night in Helena. Another tipsy patron who overheard, jumped in to defend his hero. He first accused the other man of mental clumsiness, then he called him a known thief of soiled garments from blind laundry girls, and the fight was on.

Within Montana this question became an extremely sensitive one, with some wags claiming that more persons have been killed in hindsight arguments than were slain in the actual battle. But Custer's biographers, including the newest works, all state that he was known to have been drunk on only one occasion. That single indiscretion nearly resulted in terminating the relationship with his beloved Libby. Certainly, Custer was a man with many hang-ups, and his personality was a can of worms, but alcohol was not one of his vices.

Many saloonkeepers sincerely tried to provide an interesting array of pictures to lend culture, and sometimes dignity, to their drab surroundings. In out-of-the-way frontier locations, the only art gallery most people ever saw was the one on the wall of their neighborhood saloon.

OPPOSITE: The Faure & Davies Blue Front Saloon was another in the Sam Peterson chain of drinking establishments. It stood in Breckenridge, Colorado. [Collection of Jim Andrews]

[Oil Painting by Jack Roberts]   [Ken Johnson Collection]

A GOOD STORY

Chapter 5

SALOON SOCIAL SERVICES —————————————————————————

INASMUCH AS THE LOCAL SALOON often was the only available meeting place, a rather varied assortment of social services were performed by these institutions. Lacking other facilities, many itinerant circuit-riding preachers held services in saloons. A cover was thrown over the nude paintings and the draped bar became the pulpit. And after a too-long sermon, thirsty parishoners stayed behind for a dram or two of "communion wine." Weddings and funerals were not at all uncommon in the West's thirst parlors. Once, in Nevada, when a noted gambler died, his funeral services were held in the rear of the saloon he had frequented. A fallen Methodist preacher conducted the ceremony.

When Mike Flynn died at Bear Town, Montana, his partners carried out Mike's last wish that he be buried in consecrated ground. Deer Lodge was the closest town offering such a condition. At Pioneer City the partners stopped at the saloon for a drink. One drink led to another until they realized that Flynn had not had a wake. They brought his coffin inside, set it up on beer barrels, lit some candles, and embarked on a night of drinking, singing and testimonials. They slept on the saloon floor beside the coffin and resumed their pilgrimage the next morning.

Some accommodating saloons put up whisky in small bottles labeled "medicine" for devout church people who were reluctant to do their tippling in public. When the marshal at Butte, Montana, decided to marry Mollie Dernurska, an underworld character, the nuptials were finalized in the Clipper Shades Saloon. Later, the delirious pair was "shivareed" up and down the town's main street. The newlyweds rode on the fire engine.

In frontier towns it was common for saloon-keepers to contribute money for the preacher's salary. Saturday morning was the preferred collection time. This practice gave the saloon interests an opportunity to display their civic benefactions in public and it kept the clergy from too vehement denunciations of the thirst parlors on Sunday mornings.

The saloon free lunch, a very popular social service, allegedly was first featured in New Orleans. Originally, it featured onions, crackers and cheese, rye bread, bologna, and a soup or a pot of beans. Salty foods were preferred in order to provoke thirst. In some Western saloons, you were given a brass check when you bought a beer. The check could be redeemed at the "free" lunch table, which was free only to paying customers from the bar. This practice originated with the desire of the owners to keep bums out of their premises and away from the bread and beans.

The free lunch at New York's opulent Waldorf Bar included Virginia and Westphalian ham, caviar, onions, celery, cold cuts of beef, veal and pork, rolls, and butter. The well-run Waldorf tolerated few disturbances. Among the rare breaches of the peace was the time the bibulous Buffalo Bill Cody threatened to stand nude at the bar while drinking until the management got his shirt back from a slow hotel laundry service. The shirt was procured at once!

Bartenders tend to be one of the most remembered of all facets of saloon life. They had to be philosophers, marriage counselors, encyclopedias of baseball statistics, humanitarians, and above all, sympathetic listeners. Most prided themselves in being able to concoct over a hundred rickeys, fizzes, cobblers, punches and other mixtures. But

IN AGRICULTURAL PALISADE, Colorado, this saloon
was sandwiched in-between more conventional businesses. [Collection of Richard A. Ronzio]

red liquor and beer were the staples of the trade.
Drinking on duty was an ironclad taboo. Prudent
bartenders avoided getting drawn into discussions
of religion, the merits of hanging, or the politics of
Eugene Debs. Most found it expedient to side with
the bard in the Shakespeare-Bacon dispute, perhaps because Shakespeare was known to have been
a good customer of Stratford's Mermaid Tavern,
while Bacon's drinking habits remain obscure.

Less scrupulous barkeepers in the seamier
saloons are known to have stuffed ballot boxes,
bought votes, registered votes from cemetery
rosters, rigged elections, sold booze to anyone with
the price, including unreconstructed winos and
children — and sometimes they shielded known
criminals. Saloonists often stole elections to per-
petuate their own institutions, giving rise to the

following quotation that was often repeated in the
1860's:

> I never said all Democrats were saloonkeepers;
> what I said was that all saloonkeepers were
> Democrats.

One Western saloon stated that it had two
requirements for employment of its bartenders.
These were that he must be well-armed and able to
look resolute. For "rube" customers, bartenders
set out the "cop's bottle," the cheapest "rotgut" in
the place. It is psychologically peculiar that
bartenders were blamed in part for the public
offenses committed by over-stimulated customers.
And yet nobody blamed the grocer who sold the
food to persons who died of overeating. And no

IN DENVER, Ed Starr's Saloon stood at 223 West 4th Street, between the years 1892 and 1894. The saloon dog licked up any beer that was spilled! [Collection of Jim Wright]

public outcry was raised against the jeweler who encouraged his customer to overspend, even though his excesses might also result in the man's family being deprived.

Quite apart from the social services provided by the bartender, an amazing array of other conveniences were reported in Western saloons. Sometimes, saloons provided letter boxes where good customers might receive mail. And one place maintained a depository where those who could not hold their liquor could leave their false teeth while jailed repeatedly for drunkenness. In this way, their china choppers were always available for chewing the free lunch again after they got out.

Among other social services rendered by saloons are records that most civic meetings in pioneer El Paso were held in Uncle Ben Dowell's Saloon. Dowell was the mayor. In Junction City, Kansas,

OBVERSE AND REVERSE sides of tokens from the Teller House Bar, Central City, Colorado, and the Ajax Saloon, Victor, Colorado. [Collection of Robert L. Brown]

Wells Fargo kept a file of out-of-town newspapers in the saloon as the most-frequented place where people would be most likely to see them. Job offers and help wanted ads were often posted in the corner saloon before there were any employment agencies. At Argenta, Montana, benefits held in one of the town's four saloons made it possible to raise money to pay a teacher for their three months term school. The benefits usually consisted of a public dance to raise the $60 needed.

Customer recruiting constituted no particular problem since — in the West at least — the best saloon in town was frequently the town's stage-coach station. Such facilities might be the only public place where the coaches could stop to un-load. Scarcity of safe drinking water was also a factor dictating the choice, as did the availability of public sanitary facilities. Because few homes had indoor plumbing, many saloons maintained public baths as an added social service. And, of course, every saloon was a public comfort station since few cities then provided that facility. Crea-ture comforts available in any saloon were directly related to the license fees charged by local and state revenue departments.

When Bob Fitzsimmons fought Jim Corbett at Carson City, Nevada, relays were run between the telegraph office and the saloons in towns all over the West. And as the salient blows were struck, the details were put up on a chalkboard for all to see. Gamblers raced like ferrets through tipsy crowds promoting their betting pools.

In New Orleans saloons, all sorts of business was transacted. News bulletins were posted, slaves were sold, trades were made, auctions were held and newspapermen haunted them as the best news sources. At Provo, Utah, in 1873, 21 men organ-ized a party in the Black Cat Bar to prospect in Colorado. The guide, Alferd [sic] Packer, got six of them lost in the San Juan Mountains, and the result was cannibalism — and five of the party met that fate. The fact that the party was formed in a saloon is unimportant. It probably was the only available public meeting place in Provo.

When a bank failure was rumored in Goldfield, Nevada, Tex Rickard's saloon became the deposi-tory of frightened depositors. So much cash came in that it overflowed the safe and was piled up so deep on the floor that the bartender had trouble walking around. Without hospitals, few towns could boast such a facility, medical emergencies were often brought to the saloon. Wounded men were carried in from the range, laid on a table or on the bar, and "doctored" with whisky while broken bones were set or bullets were removed. Saloon women wiped perspiring brows, and most of the patients pulled through. In a gambling environment, the whole process took on added interest as bets were laid and odds given on the patients' chances of recovery or death.

Sometimes, as in Seattle or Cheyenne, saloons were a stimulus to growth. But there were at least two cases where saloons caused towns to relocate. At Old Congress Town, on the southern slope of Red Mountain Pass, local history insists that when the saloonkeeper moved his stock up to a prettily located open meadow on the top of the pass, the whole thirsty population followed along. The result was the founding of Red Mountain Town. Later there were several saloons there with names like Assembly Club and the Miner's Delight. By 1880, the census recorded 10,000 people at Red Moun-tain Town, a ridiculous figure that may have reflected the interest of census takers in the local dram shops.

The original location of Placerville, Colorado, was at the point where the highway starts south along the San Miguel River toward Telluride. But when the local saloon was moved to a new building a mile south, Placerville pulled up its roots and clustered around the new location. Not a stick remains at its former site.

The towns of Arland and Meteetsee, in northern

Wyoming, were founded with the sole purpose of supplying Montana and Wyoming rangehands with women and liquor. Carousing, it was hoped, would occur in these places and away from the abodes of more-civilized persons. In Arland, the only businesses were the bordello, called a "hotel," a dancehall, store and post office.

Northwestern logging operations were mostly owned and operated by stern New England people who cherished negative notions about the ravages of liquor on their work gangs. So, in their off-duty hours, the men sought places like Seattle, which grew up around a saloon, where they could drink and socialize with fine young Klamath and Cayuse Indian girls. That first saloon was named Ilahee, and was founded by John Pennell, a veteran of San Francisco's Barbary Coast saloon circuit.

Cheyenne, Wyoming, was a railroad town that grew as a direct outgrowth of the Union Pacific construction schedule in 1869. Cheyenne's first saloon arrived that year, fully assembled and ready to operate, shipped to town on a railroad flatcar. The same building had been used in Julesburg, Colorado, once called the toughest town in the West. Wild throngs of gandy dancers and other railroad workers found their most familiar haunts there, at Cheyenne's end-of-track, ready for business as usual. Gamblers, hurdy-gurdy girls, dancehall operators and other camp followers were not far behind.

And sometimes, miners slept on saloon floors at the end of a boom. When the Sherman Silver Purchase Act was repealed in 1893, impoverished men with no jobs spread newspapers on the saloon floor at Granite, Montana, and huddled together for warmth. But in pioneer Goldfield, Nevada, and Leadville, Colorado, the shortage of any shelter produced the same result, and people paid to sleep on barroom floors after closing time. In many places, this phenomenon was repeated at the start of a gold rush, in the days before hotel construction could meet local demand.

With the passage of years, quite a large number of well-known persons have come to be associated with saloons in one capacity or another. Abraham Lincoln was exposed briefly to a career as a saloonkeeper. At New Salem, Illinois, in March of 1833, Lincoln and his partner, William F. Berry, took out a license to sell a variety of brandies, wine, gin, rum and whisky. Although Lincoln himself was an abstainer, the tavern license was used as a way of making his grocery store pay its way. In later years, copies of Lincoln's license were prominently displayed in saloons all across the United States.

The incredibly talented Victor Herbert — source of so many marvelous operettas — drank huge steins of Pilsener beer at the Grand Union Hotel bar in Saratoga, New York. In one popular story — probably untrue — we are told that he wrote most of the musical score and libretto for *Mlle. Modiste* on these premises. In the years immediately preceding the Civil War, Steven Foster composed many of his most famous songs in a saloon at Chrystie and Hester streets in New York City. Various publishers purchased them for amounts up to $25. Before he died in 1864, he had turned out 77 songs while sustaining life on beer and raw vegetables. Twenty-nine of his compositions were hymns.

Andrew Jackson, John W. ("Bet-a-Million") Gates, Wild Bill Hickok, U.S. Grant, William Randolph Hearst and William F. ("Buffalo Bill") Cody, were frequent saloon visitors. In Cody's case, there are at least 11 different saloon versions of his epic duel with Chief Yellow Hand at Summit Springs. All came from Denver saloons and all are attributed to Cody. The accounts seem to vary according to what he was drinking and the quantity he had consumed at the time the story was being told. Once, after visiting a saloon, Cody rode his horse onto the stage of the Tabor Grand Opera House, interrupting — according to one version — Act III of *Macbeth*. Cody's favorite

OBVERSE AND REVERSE sides of tokens from Joe Bryant's Saloon, Robinson, Colorado, and the White Front Saloon, Raton, New Mexico. [Collection of Robert L. Brown]

THESE WELL-DRESSED GENTLEMEN are standing at the handsome bar of Leadville's Topic Saloon. Note the tall spittoons and the heavily pomaded bartender. [Collection of Jim Andrews]

drink was called a Stone Fence. It consisted of a shot of rye whisky in a glass of cider with a lemon peel. When offered a drink, his favorite retort was, "Sir, you speak the language of my tribe."

Many ex-boxers, including a few champions like Jack Dempsey and a few near-misses like Tony Galento, drifted into barkeeping or the restaurant business. Others included John L. Sullivan, whose remarkable thirst has become almost legendary. He drank several saloon partners into bankruptcy and finally ended in bankruptcy court himself.

U.S. Grant's drinking was partly confined to his pre-Civil War era in California, when this habit led to his resignation from the Army, under pressure. Grant was lonely, and when his beloved wife, Julie, was present he stayed sober. President Lincoln was aware of Grant's weakness and provision was made to keep Mrs. Grant nearby during the war years. When Grant's enemies told Lincoln about the drinking, he is alleged to have suggested that they find out what Grant drank so he could include it in the rations of his less-aggressive generals! The Grant saloon patronage also occurred during his years at Galion, Ohio. All things considered, Grant was a much finer man than one would think from the image that his name projects today. Although he was a far-from-great president, he was a very capable commander and one of the few who would stand and fight the Confederates.

Sometimes, leaders of a community who lacked office space made their headquarters in a saloon. James Butler "Wild Bill" Hickok made his office in the back of a bordello and was murdered in the saloon. His assassin, and most of Deadwood's residents, knew that their marshal could nearly always be found at the grog shop.

Eugene Field was one of the rarest and most-original gems who ever worked among Denver's newspapers. Widely known as a practical joker, Field deflated pompous local politicians (H.A.W. Tabor was a favorite target), frustrated the rather pathetic "400" of Denver's society crowd, and turned the Colorado lecture tour of Oscar Wilde into a local joke of marvelous complexity. Field conceived, and successfully carried out, a public impersonation of Wilde, capitalizing on the most-obvious aspects of Oscar's well-known effeminacy.

Field also enjoyed his liquor and regarded local temperance laws as a personal affront. Gold Hill was a mining town in Boulder County where miners had rejected saloons by popular vote. Field enjoyed the huge old Goldminer Hotel and took perverse satisfaction from smuggling liquor into the town and consuming it in his room at the hotel. Local folklore (but not history) makes much of the story that Field wrote some of his finest poetry for children while intoxicated in the hotel of this temperance town. At Gold Hill — now almost a ghost town — owners of the hotel proudly show a woven wicker table on which Field allegedly wrote.

Sam Houston — he of gigantic thirst — having won a victory in a local election, became so elated that he began hitting the saloons to celebrate. As the late historian Lucius Beebe told the story in Denver one night, "The result was a gargantuan drunk, in the course of which Houston stripped to the skin, threw his clothing into a public bonfire, and danced stark-naked through the streets."

In the War of 1812, Andrew Jackson planned his brilliant defense against the British in a New Orleans saloon, the Exchange, on St. Louis Street. It was built and operated by Pierre Maspero. It had a dirt floor and fancy brass spittoons, in common with most saloons of that time. Ethan Allen and his Green Mountain boys, who — with the invaluable help of Benedict Arnold — captured Fort Ticonderoga, had imbibed freely at Steven Fay's Catamount Tavern in Bennington, Vermont, just before the attack. They drank hot rum, and most of the men were drunk when they attacked. Some of their zeal came almost assuredly from the Catamount.

Even General George Washington was not above capitalizing on the alcoholic habits of his enemies. When he crossed the ice-filled Delaware River on December 26, he knew full well that the Hessians would be sleeping off the effects of their typical Christmas celebrating. He attacked, won a great victory, and swept on to Princeton.

Energetic, non-conforming Teddy Roosevelt — one of the few truly brilliant American Presidents — was a participant in one of the most-publicized saloon brawls of all time. Following the death of Alice, his first wife, the adventurous Roosevelt went West to put his life back together on a Dakota cattle ranch. After one particularly hard day in the saddle, Teddy took care of his horse and entered the saloon of the town's only hotel. Allegedly, Teddy ordered coffee. The village bully, already drunk and profane, took offense at Roosevelt's choice of drink and loudly ordered "four-eyes" to set up drinks for the house. Ignored, the huge cowboy staggered over and repeated the order. Although T. R. was physically small, he had been the champion boxer for his weight at Harvard. Slowly, deliberately, he rose from his chair, removed his thick glasses, and drove home two fast punches that sent the now-unconscious man crashing into the bar. Other customers threw the man out and the saloonkeeper ordered free drinks on the house. It was this event, most biographers agree, that won Teddy the acceptance he had hoped for among his Western neighbors.

Theodore Roosevelt, as a young candidate for the General Assembly of New York state, sought votes in local saloons. And during the Spanish-American War, Lt. Colonel Theodore Roosevelt trained the 1st Volunteer Cavalry at an Army post in Texas. Following one particularly satisfactory exercise, Teddy treated his Rough Riders to all the beer they could hold in a San Antonio saloon. But military rules frowned on fraternization between officers and their men. Army brass hats fumed, probably remembering that Mark Hanna had not been able to control the unpredictable Roosevelt either. Reporters made it worse by giving the story wide distribution. The public loved it, but military traditionalists choked over their cherished caste system being flaunted in a common saloon.

All things considered, the physical places where men drank were probably more important in the development of the American West than the actual drinking. A student in need of a subject for a Master's thesis could likely build a study around the sociology of the saloon and its effect on Western history without ever probing very deeply into the drinking aspects of its customers.

[Oil Painting by Jack Roberts]   [Neil Mincer Collection]

THE TOAST

Chapter 6
MINING-CAMP SALOONS ————————————————————

IT WAS NOT THE DOLLARS-AND-CENTS VALUE of the precious metals extracted from the earth in 19th-Century America that brought about the populating of the West, but rather it was the presence of the gold seeker. True, it was the rumor of silver or gold in a depression-ridden United States that sparked the mass migration that sent thousands of persons tumbling into California and Nevada. But their lifestyles, evolving institutions, and the way they faced their problems were of greater importance in the westward movement than the things they sought.

Of all the thousands of drinking establishments that flourished in the American West, those that grew up and flourished in our mountain mining camps probably were the most colorful. One prospector was quoted as saying, "I once spent a week in Virginia City's saloons one night."

In mining towns, the number of operating saloons was regarded as a yardstick of prosperity and an index of the number of employed miners. Kokomo, Colorado, bragged that it had a hundred operating saloons along Ten Mile Avenue in 1881. Early-day guide books usually listed the number of saloons, general stores, churches, banks and railroads as a town's most-conspicuous status symbols. The existence of "bit" and "two-bit" saloons degraded a town's image. Sometimes the number of bars reached the saturation point, and in the competition for trade that followed, the consumer might enjoy a band, a price war, or prostitutes used as bait to attract the customer through the swinging doors. Gambling sometimes helped, too. Faro, roulette, three-card monte, craps, and draw and stud poker were the favorites. Some preferred dice games, commonly known as "African golf," at that time.

While standing with one foot on the brass rail, men told and retold tall stories about mining personalities and unusual events that have since become legends. Their conversations covered exceptional luck while gambling, funny tales about the drinking capacity of this or that miner, Herculean feats of strength or bravery, superstitious beliefs of miners about "Tommy-Knockers," the effects of women underground or near mines, and blow-by-blow accounts of great fist fights.

In Colorado's Gilpin County, partly true stories of an illiterate Irish miner named Pat Casey are still popular. In Wyoming's Grand Encampment district they told stories of a prospector whose arms were so long that he could lace his boots without even bending over. And in Eureka, Nevada, they related tales of a powerful-and-fleet-footed miner who could throw a bottle of whisky high into the air above the saloon, then race around the building in time to catch it in the alley.

The comparative ratio between saloons and population tend to be much quoted, mostly because such statistics seem to confirm our stereotyped ideas about life in the West. For example, in 1906, Rhyolite, Nevada, had 16,000 inhabitants and 45 saloons. This would amount to a saloon for each 360 people — men, women and children — who lived and worked at Rhyolite.

At the same time, Rhyolite supported only two churches, one Presbyterian, the other Catholic. And sometimes overlooked were cultural groups that did, in fact, exert some influence. The Women's Rhyolite Society planned bazaars, dances and charity benefits for the family-type people in the town. There was a school, too, but nobody had

AT RED MOUNTAIN, Colorado, the Miner's Delight and the Red Mountain tent-saloon were open during the town's earliest days. [Collection of Robert L. Brown]

thought to hire a teacher the first year.

In the Northern Saloon of Goldfield, Nevada, a dozen bartenders sold six barrels of whisky each day across what was billed as the world's longest bar. Tex Rickard, a sometimes fight-promoter who spent far more time in Alaska and Nevada than in Texas, was the owner of the Northern. One doorway and some stonework from one wall are all that remain of the place now. And there was a plush saloon in the $500,000 Goldfield Hotel. When it opened on Columbia Avenue in 1910, champagne flowed through the lobby and was allowed to run down the steps into the street. Goldfield's stray dogs had a tipsy field day in the gutters. Although closed for many years, the Goldfield Hotel was reopened as a brothel in 1972. This "profession" has long been legal by local option in some Nevada counties. The red-plush carpets and red-velvet drapes seem somehow appropriate to the Goldfield's rebirth. Further

down the block, four saloons occupied the four corners where Crook and Main streets intersected. These were the Northern, the Palace, the Mohawk and the Hermitage, and they all stayed open 24 hours a day.

In pioneer Austin, Nevada, no tree, flower or blade of grass could be found. But gold and silver had been found in 1862, and a number of saloons were in full swing before the first summer had passed. One of them placed the following advertisement in Austin's daily paper:

Mammoth Lager Beer Saloon, in the basement, corner of Main and Virginia streets, Austin, Nevada. Choice liquors, wines, lager beer and cigars served by pretty girls, who understand their business and attend to it. . .

While miners bellied up to the bars in the many saloons at Virginia City, the boom of explosives often was heard, and ornately embossed bar bottles — perched precariously on narrow shelves —

AT LAWSON, COLORADO, the prominently located saloon also sported a sign on the back of its building.
[Collection of Richard A. Ronzio]

shivered with every blast. Mark Twain, who sometimes exaggerated, said that there was "... a whisky mill every 15 steps, a dozen breweries and a dozen jails." Mark Twain also defined a mine as, "a hole in the ground owned by a liar." Two former San Francisco saloon proprietors, James C. Flood and William S. O'Brien, put up the money for John W. Mackay and James G. Fair. By the 1870's these four men controlled the Comstock Lode and formed the powerful Consolidated Virginia holdings.

In lawless Tombstone, Arizona, saloon and gambling dens along Allen Street kept their swinging doors open around the clock. Bar girls at Ed Schieffelin's bar and theatre sang as they hustled booze to the customers. Old-timers insist that two of every three businesses were saloons or gambling halls. Its Bird Cage Theatre and Saloon never closed while the boom lasted. It was open around the clock.

Mining-town saloons were often large tents. Sometimes they had slab-side walls with a canvas roof stretched over the top. In many instances the facility was shared with a barber shop and grocery store. The result was bedlam for customers and clerks. To further enhance the madness, bibulous members of the local amateur quartet could be heard practicing at the bar. Double doors hung on many saloons in country where heavy snows blanketed high-altitude Western towns. A large set of full-length double doors kept the winter inclemencies outside from November through April. During the summer, the larger doors were folded away against the walls and the more conventional swinging doors were employed. For some peculiar reason, the saloon at Nevada City, Montana, hung its swinging doors outside the others, fully exposed during bad weather.

In prosperous mining towns, it became customary for saloons to set up the first free drinks when

OBVERSE AND REVERSE of tokens from the B&F Bar, Elizabeth, Colorado, and Joh Bitzer's Bank Bar, Leadville, Colorado. [Collection of Robert L. Brown]

a shift of miners came out of the pits. Often the first drink in the morning was a free one, and some miners made the rounds of a dozen or more saloons before reporting for their work shift.

Occasionally, a mining town in a remote location would exhaust its supply of liquid refreshments. Such was the case at Silver City, Idaho, in February of 1866. *The Owyhee Avalanche* then printed this item:

> According to an old woman's saying that "bread is the staff of life, but whisky is life itself," we are out of "life" right now, but there is flour enough to meet present needs.

One brewery in town kited the Indian name and made "Owyhee Beer."

Idaho City, east of Boise, had 4 breweries and 41 saloons, including the Buena Vista, which was accessible to thirsty miners by way of a swinging foot bridge across Elk Creek. It was a satisfactory bridge when men were sober, but the swinging and rocking produced some interesting resolutions from intoxicated patrons. Some chose to drink in the Miner's Exchange in the future to avoid that undulating suspended span. Others preferred John Cody's Saloon at Main and Wall streets. Cody's was the source of the destructive 1867 fire that left Idaho City in ashes.

In Auburn, Oregon, a miner named French Pete was placed on trial in a saloon before a hastily assembled jury of his peers. They found him guilty of mixing strychnine in with his partner's flour. As with miners' courts, "justice" was swift. French Pete "died of a stoppage of the breath caused when the platform on which he was standing suddenly gave way." The location is still known as Gallows Hill. After observing a saloon-convened miners' court in Nevada, Mark Twain observed that he "... had never seen a court that functioned so quickly nor one that carried out its edicts with so little nonsense."

Early-day accounts of the California Gold Rush of 1849 nearly always included references to the sailing ships that clogged San Francisco harbor. Because the crews had deserted to go in search of gold, the schooners were unable to sail away. The eventual disposition of these hulks is a unique American success story. Many of them were converted to floating saloons and chained to the piers. The original ship's name became the name of the saloon.

When Bodie, California, boomed, there was no wood. All lumber had to be hauled-in from the Sierras. Saloons were among the first structures. When 20-foot snowdrifts covered the town, the mines closed for the winter. One miner wrote, "... there's nothing to do but hang around the saloons, get drunk and fight." Conditions presumably returned to normal. Saloon killings were common. Two drunken miners stepped into the alley after much bragging over the bar about their marksmanship. Bodie's citizens celebrated a double funeral the next day. An 1855 California newspaper reported "... those worse than fiends rush, vulture-like, upon the scene and erect a round tent, wherein are gambling, drinking, swearing and fighting; the many reproduce pandemonium in more than its original horror."

Saloons could be ego boosters, too, particularly for the big spenders. Gambler Nate Arnold grew rich from a chance gold discovery. He hired a brass band and put on a one-man parade through the saloon district of Columbia, California. He often marched into Long Tom's Bar and paid with $20 gold pieces. That was his standard price for a drink. No change was requested, and his ego got a lift. When his mine failed and Nate was down on his luck, none of the bartenders who had sold him drinks at fancy prices came forward to help. He died poor and was buried at county expense.

Cerrillos, northeast of Albuquerque, New Mexico, grew up in 1879 around the San Pedro gold, silver and copper mines. Indian stone axes and turquoise were present in the ancient mine shafts.

Twenty-one saloons served the 2,500 residents. Best-known among the thirst-quenchers was the Tiffany Saloon, started in 1860, when the New York jewelry firm had an interest in the turquoise deposits there. Both food and liquor were served across a 22-foot-long walnut bar. A traditional brass foot-rail of the same length helped customers keep their balance while standing to drink. A theatre of modest size was behind the barroom. At the turn of the century, Thomas A. Edison tried using static electricity to gather the fine gold dust particles at Cerrillos. He failed, but his presence in the town was fine publicity.

At Cimarron, New Mexico, the saloons were in the Maxwell House and Saint James Hotel. The latter was run by Henry Lambert, one-time chef of President Lincoln. Allegedly, 28 killings occurred in the Saint James. When Pancho Griego killed three Negro soldiers there, it inflated his ego. He provoked an argument with the infamous Clay Allison, hiding his gun behind his sombrero. Allison saw through the ploy and plugged Griego twice through the head before Pancho could bring his gun into play. Local citizens, hardened to instant death, would say, "Lambert had a man for breakfast," whenever there was a murder at the Saint James. *The Las Vegas Gazette* once noted that, "Everything is quiet in Cimarron. Nobody has been killed for three days."

A similarly blase attitude was evident in pioneer Leadville, Colorado. Street and saloon killings became so common that one newspaper carried a black bordered column titled Breakfast Bullets that listed the names of men who had died violently the day before.

Business directories for the years of the Leadville silver excitement list more than 150 saloons on Harrison, State and Chestnut streets. A man in search of pleasure during Leadville's boom, had a choice of many types of saloons, plus 115 gambling dens — and some other establishments where he could dispose of his money rapidly. But there were few hotels. And when the frightful cold of this above-10,000-foot-high location set-in, human suffering was great. Flophouses did a flourishing business at 50 cents a body. Other people crowded the saloons for shelter and drank all night. The practice of sleeping on the floors of gambling houses and saloons was common. At closing time, a bar boy took chalk in hand and marked off the rough plank floor into rectangles, each barely large enough to accommodate a body. Fifty cents per space per night was the price as the floor was thrown open for guests. Those who had them, spread their blankets on the floor. Most removed wet shoes and socks, and draped them over the rafters. Their rolled-up coats served as pillows while they shivered through an eight-hour shift.

Notorious Blair Street in Silverton, Colorado, had in excess of 40 saloons, gambling dens and sporting houses. While the number of "girls" employed varied during enforcement and protection eras, between 200 and 300 found employment of a sort here. Bat Masterson was once hired to clean up Blair Street. He failed. Local wags insist that the great gunman succumbed to the street's enticing blandishments and enjoyed himself thoroughly while on the town payroll. Most of Blair Street's buildings that escaped the fire still stand. Others, perpetuating the false front-boardwalk motif, have been constructed. During the past two decades Blair Street has been discovered by Hollywood and several shoot-'em-up Westerns have been filmed here.

In 1860, William Hepworth Dixon, an English cleric, visited Denver and found it a town of 4,000 people where, "Every fifth house appears to be a bar, a whisky-shop, a lager beer saloon; every tenth house appears to be either a brothel or a gambling house; very often both in one."

Denver's earliest full-service saloon was a log structure, single level, over 100 feet in length and

OBVERSE AND REVERSE sides of tokens from King's Saloon, French Gulch, California, and the Last Chance Saloon, Jackson, Wyoming. [Collection of Robert L. Brown]

NOT EVERYONE went to the saloons. Some, like this
miner, operated their own stills. [Western History Collection—Denver Public Library]

35 feet wide. It was called the Denver House. It
had a sod floor, glassless windows and an unfinished pine bar. Horace Greeley, owner of *The
New York Telegraph*, gave a temperance speech in
the Denver House. He cautioned against drinking,
gambling and consorting with lewd women. He was
cheered lustily, and then all three activities were
resumed as soon as he had gone. He spent the
night in the almost-equally-rowdy Elephant Corral,
Denver's first hotel, but was unable to sleep.
Raucous laughter, booming guns and gambling
noises penetrated the burlap walls. But Horace was
tenacious. He gave almost the same speech a few
nights later to the miners in Gregory Gulch, was
again cheered vigorously; however, no one was ever
accused of following his advice. Pine-knot torches
illuminated the crowd that sat on the hillside to
hear Greeley.

Before the fire in April of 1896, there were 50
gambling houses and saloons along Bennett Ave-

nue in Cripple Creek — in just the three blocks
between Second and Fifth streets. The late Claude
Miner of Golden, Colorado, once told a story
passed on by his father, the editor of *The Animas
Forks Pioneer*. Animas Forks was located in a
valley, the elevation of which was well above 11,000
feet, and snowslides sometimes buried the town
under drifts 25 feet deep. On such occasions, work
in the mines was suspended while tunnels were dug
from homes to business houses. Curiously —
according to Mr. Miner — most of the tunnels
seemed to lead to Alfred Sam's Alamo Saloon.

When the western Montana and Idaho mining
rushes hit their stride in 1864 and '65, Virginia
City and Nevada City in Alder Gulch had four
hurdy-gurdies that stayed open every night. Idaho
City had several and they could be found in nearly
all of the Black Hills towns. At Sterling, Montana,
a substantial amount of gold dust was recovered by
panning the dirt under the floors of the town's

SLEEPERS RENTED "BODY SPACES" in gambling halls and saloons during mining rushes. This photograph was taken at Goldfield, Nevada. [Collection of Fred and Jo Mazzulla]

several saloons after Sterling had become a ghost town.

When the Northern Pacific Railroad established Forsythe, Montana, as an end-of-track town in the 1880's, a dozen pre-fab saloons were brought in on flatcars. They were assembled and in full operation within the first day — and one shooting had already taken place in a fight over a dancehall girl. The dancehall was presumably prefabricated and shipped-in on the same train.

On the average, most Westerners who imbibed, consumed five to six whiskys daily. In the larger gold and silver camps, there was a saloon of some sort for each hundred or so men. Allegedly, a Butte, Montana, town character known as "Callahan the Bum" claimed to know 57 different ways to bum a drink.

A substantial gold rush took people from the states into the province of British Columbia in 1858, when Billy Barker found the yellow metal in what was to become the famous Cariboo Mining District. Its center was the town of Barkerville, once touted as being the largest community north of San Francisco and west of Chicago. *The Cariboo Sentinel* reported 12 saloons along the Cariboo Wagon Road, which became the town's principal street. Here, as elsewhere, some saloons were respectable, while others were rowdy. At one time, gambling was outlawed in all Barkerville saloons.

Among the thirst-quenchers, one could find some unusual names like the Gazelle Parlor, Go-At-Them, Barry & Adler's Fashion, The Snug, and the inevitable Crystal Palace. Special entertainment ran to boxing matches and magic shows. When such events were booked, seats in the saloons sold for $2 each, but on regular evenings, there was no "cover charge."

Although not so productive of quick wealth as the precious-metal towns, there were also communities where other elements were extracted from the earth. Life was hard and dismal, and the saloons that catered to their needs were among the

THE EVERGREEN SALOON is shown in the extreme left
of this view. It was located in the short-lived community
of Park City, Colorado—near the Adelaide mine in Stray
Horse Gulch, about a mile east of Leadville. [Library,
State Historical Society of Colorado]

most cheerless in North America. Turn-of-the-century coal-mining towns, less numerous than those where gold or silver were sought, had a full complement of saloons.

Company officials controlled the towns, acted as mayors and determined who ran the company store, who could teach in the school, and even the churches were under the corporate thumb. In "closed" towns, barbed wire fenced the entire area and armed camp-marshals patrolled the private road that was the only way in or out. So, company-controlled saloons were nothing unusual, and not many miners did their imbibing in the privately owned bistros that flourished in the towns nearby.

In coal-town saloons, the off-duty miner not only sought relaxation, the place was also the center for labor recruitment. Company-owned saloons were also espionage posts. "Spotters," as corporate spies

were called, gathered here, fraternized with the men and listened for dangerous loose talk about such taboo subjects as unionization, the eight-hour day or guaranteed hourly wages. Often, there was a magazine rack containing *Judge, Life, The Saturday Evening Post* or *Camp and Plant*. However, publications like *The Police Gazette* and *Harpers Weekly*, which contained revolutionary writing by reformers like Upton Sinclair, were unwelcome.

Saloonkeepers leased the land on which their establishment was constructed. Like the customers they served, they, too, existed at the pleasure of coal company officials. Little rowdyism was tolerated. One saloonkeeper saw his lease terminated, not by a court, but by the company, when he purchased liquor from an "unfriendly" supplier. Then, there was the language barrier. Turn-of-the-century coal miners' towns were a mixture of

THREE PIECES of saloon art are visible above the gambling table in this Van Wyck, Idaho, saloon. [Courtesy Idaho Historical Society]

OBVERSE AND REVERSE sides of tokens from Tom Connor's Bank Saloon, Hamilton, Ohio, and the Montana Saloon, Helena, Montana. [Collection of Robert L. Brown]

Austrians, Germans, Mexicans, Irish, Yugoslavians, Italians, Poles and Welshmen. Few bartenders could satisfactorily perform the usual functions under such handicaps.

If they understood English, there were better jobs for America's immigrants. If not, there was work as a "gandy dancer," pick-and-shovel jobs, the Chicago stockyards, or there was always coal mining. On election days, coal company officials came to the saloons to help the miners mark their ballots, while the barroom continued to function in the usual way. In Colorado's Huerfano County, there were 45 coal-town saloons, and they all belonged to the Spanish Peaks Mercantile Company.

But even in coal-mining locations, there were occasional operators with an eye toward progress. One unusual saloon was opened at Redstone, Colorado, in 1900. Benevolent John Cleveland Osgood built a model town in the Crystal River Valley. Miners' cottages were painted a variety of pastel colors. An Osgood school, a church and an opera house soon appeared. But it was the saloon

SALOON ART at the Shanahan & Haggerty establishment in Idaho City included a stuffed bear holding a bottle. The date was 1915. [Courtesy Idaho Historical Society]

that really made people sit up and take notice. Since Osgood believed that strong drink lowered both moral fiber and work capacity, the "clubhouse," as it was called, was controlled by his Colorado Fuel & Iron Company. It was built to look like a Swiss chalet, and the formal opening was a magnificent public ball. A permanent "no treating" rule was rigidly enforced.

And so it went — all across the Western landscape. Wherever there was a hole in the ground, people congregated. Sometimes, established towns resulted, while in other places, it was just an informal settlement. But in almost all cases, incorporated or not, one of the first business ventures was a saloon.

OPPOSITE, ABOVE and BELOW: The upper photograph shows the backroom beer-barrel storage area of one of the Sam Peterson saloons, while the lower view portrays gambling tables that were standard fixtures in most saloons belonging to this chain. [Collection of Jim Andrews]

[Oil Painting by Jack Roberts]   [Ken Johnson Collection]

BELLE OF THE BAR

Chapter 7
CATTLE-COUNTRY SALOONS ———————————————

THE WEST'S OPEN-RANGE CATTLE ERA lasted less than two decades. Completion of the transcontinental railroads placed wheels under cash and credit, and rolled artificial refrigeration cars west across the wide Missouri. Better markets after the Civil War were also factors, as was the development of the tin can. These three reasons took the local butcher out of butchering in the early 1870's and brought to prominence the cowboy — probably the most appealing folk hero yet to emerge on the American scene.

Two considerations probably account for the vast public interest in cowboys. One was the increase in literate persons needing something to read after Horace Mann broke his health in establishing public schools. The other was the skill of contemporary writers in producing stories about cowboys, the most exciting heroes of the moment. The pattern, once established, has persisted. Westerns are still our most popular brand of fiction. They were the favorite reading matter of President Eisenhower, and of thousands of other people. Detective stories are a not-too-close second. And Western movies still account for a substantial majority of the feature films we export to the rest of the world.

Most of the cattle towns were in Kansas, Nebraska, Wyoming and the Dakotas. As the railroad moved west, the end-of-the-line towns in Kansas were successively Abilene, Ellsworth, Newton, Wichita, Hays City and Dodge City. In Colorado, Julesburg and Trail City were cattle towns. And when the long drives north from Texas reached their destination after months on the trail, cowboys had money in their pockets and headed for the nearest town's "Texas Street," the saloon district.

Some of them drank too much, fought in the streets, and occasionally they rode their horses through the swinging doors to the bar, demanding that their animals be served beers. Sometimes they shot revolvers in the air. Most were poor marksmen, but a few shot out the hanging oil lamps. Now and then, they whooped and yelled, and rode horses up and down the wooden sidewalks, but most of their "hoorahing the town" was harmless. "Paper-collared Comanches" was a favorite name that cowboys called saloonkeepers. There was little love lost between the two groups. Most "Texas Street" businessmen were devoted to the principle that the cowboy's money, being heavy and a burden, should not remain in the pockets of his jeans long enough to impede his progress to camp.

Cowboys — like saloons and cows — are not particularly new, although many people tend to regard the man on horseback as a uniquely American product. The term "cowboy" was first used on Irish cattle ranches around the year 1,000 A.D. Irish prisoners brought the word to Massachusetts Bay in 1640 during the Puritan Revolution. Cattle-tenders who herded John Pyncheon's cattle between Boston and Springfield in 1655 were known as cowboys. Mexican *vaqueros* added boots, chaps, broad-brimmed hats and hundreds of the most-used words now associated with cowboys. For example, the word "ranch" originally designated a *vaquero* nickname for beef stew. The barbecue came from Mexico by way of the West Indies where, in the 1700's, it was first used to describe a cookery technique for preparing a roast enemy.

America's first cowtown saloon was in New

REGAN BAY'S JUNCTION SALOON was a popular spot
in Creede, Colorado. [State Historical Society of Colo-
rado]

York's Bowery and was called the Bull's Head. It was a stockmen's headquarters in the early 18th Century. Two others were the De Lancey on Cherry Street and the Noah's Ark on Stuyvesant Street. Bull-baitings and target-shooting were held in all three places.

As the railroad was built across Kansas, a whole succession of end-of-track towns came to life. While on the trail, cattle outfits often camped across the river from a town. The river was for watering the animals and the town was for watering the men. After supper, those not on duty would ford the river and carouse for a few hours. Saloons, gambling houses and brothels were the only sources of entertainment so the men naturally drifted into them. Doubtless, some of the men would have looked for better entertainment if it

had been available. Unmarried, unchurched, unschooled and frequently unwashed, cowboys just off the trail spent their time in the wrong part of town, frustrating the efforts of church groups and Eastern temperance societies.

Both the quality and quantity of liquor were apt to be secondary considerations. Some other, but not as widely used facilities, were the churches, restricted by sect or creed, and literary societies, in a time when many Westerners were illiterate. Saloons, gambling houses and brothels overlooked these restrictions and never closed during cattle shipping seasons, because, "nobody shoots Santa Claus." Beginning in 1877, the number of cattle-town saloons tripled. Some of the older ones, like the famed Long Branch, competed with each other to see which would be the most elegant. And in the

AT BRECKENRIDGE, Colorado, the National Saloon stood on the west side of the town's main street. [State Historical Society of Colorado]

same town, cowboys found the Gay Lady and the Comique. And behind the saloons and dancehalls, stood rows of two-room cabins, erected for immoral purposes.

In the cowtowns of Kansas, the saloons were given names reflecting the heritage of their Texas customers, Lone Star, Alamo, Houston and Austin, were popular. Among cattle towns, Abilene was the first. It was divided into a law-abiding half and a "Devil's Half Acre," frequented by Texas cowboys "in search of the elephant." Drunkenness and murders were common in the Bull Head Saloon, just down the street. In the notorious Bull Head, the proprietor kept the ladies out and shocked a few male customers when he put up a life-size four-color portrait of a huge bull, equipped with certain highly exaggerated biological features.

In Abilene, cowboys were allowed in town, but an ordinance restricted their presence to "Devil's Half Acre." Any "cattle farmers" found on the streets of the law-abiding, decent part of town were subject to instant arrest during the latter years of Abilene's prominence as a cattle community.

In Abilene an intoxicated cowboy once rode from the saloon to the barber shop, maneuvered his horse through the door, drew his gun and forced the barber to climb up on a chair and shave him while he remained on the horse. After Abilene was cleaned up in 1872, it lost its identity as a cowtown, and was replaced by Ellsworth, Newton, Wichita, Hays City, Dodge City and a score of others.

Each year in the spring, scores of girls flocked into the cattle towns with the singular mission of selling themselves for as much as possible, and as often as possible, before the cowboys went home. Most succeeded admirably.

Abilene's cowboy district was just south of the railroad tracks. During the period of the cattle drives, the street was dust-clogged. It was filled with cowboys, cattle, farmers and local businessmen. But at 4:00 p.m., business came to a standstill as local streetwalkers came out to promenade along the broad sidewalks. This was a daily happening. The girls walked in groups and did a bit of personal advertising.

To avoid hassles that could not be controlled, considering the size of the local constabulary, the city fathers set aside an area surrounded by a high stockade fence as a red-light district. For the personal convenience of these same city fathers, the area was adjacent to the business district. Inside the fence, a dozen or so big army-barracks-like structures housed the local talent. And, of course, gambling halls and saloons separated the barracks.

Saloons with "red-light" overtones tended to congregate in certain areas, usually on the outer fringe of a town, probably to insure more-effective policing. In Abilene, the tenderloin area was known as McCoy's Addition, or the Beer Garden. Newton's "houses" were clustered in Hide Park, while Ellsworth sported its Nauchville, or "town of the night." In Wichita, it was called Delano, or West Wichita.

Physically, a majority of the buildings bore striking similarities. Most were one or two-story frame structures, long and narrow. On the main floor was the dance area, with a raised platform in the corner for a trio of musicians or a piano banger. Extending down the longest wall was the bar. Behind it, or beside it, was the liquor-storage cabinet or a deep ice chest. Adjacent to the dancing area, a long hall extended for the full length of the building. On both sides of this corridor were tiny rooms where the bar girls could perform their "horizontal work" in privacy. Within Dodge City one could find several of these establishments just a block from the main business district.

Each madame paid a license fee, was assured of police protection, and agreed to keep the girls inside, except for occasional shopping trips. From the suburbs, a shuttle service of hacks ran on a regular schedule to the vice district.

In Kansas, during cattle days, nearly any place could serve as a saloon-dancehall-brothel. There are records of these functions being performed in dugouts, on snowbound trains, in tepees, soddies, wagons, on moving freight trains and even on the

CANADIAN AND AMERICAN tastes in barroom art were markedly similar. This is the restored House Hotel Bar at Barkerville, British Columbia. [Collection of Robert L. Brown]

open prairie. Portable brothels on wheels, called cat wagons, traveled from town to town with cattle drives. The authorities at Fort Dodge were particularly plagued by these horse-drawn prairie parlor houses.

Curiously, even the toughest cowboys assumed a chivalrous attitude in the presence of women — any women! Wives and daughters of Kansas citizens walked the streets unmolested. In early Abilene, no respectable woman was ever bothered on the streets, perhaps because the town sported more saloons, gambling dens and brothels than

KELLEY'S SALOON in the Cariboo District, at Barkerville, British Columbia. [Collection of Robert L. Brown]

stores. There were 20 in one single block. The local directory for 1871 showed 32 liquor outlets, 64 gambling tables and 134 known gamblers. In Newton, every other business featured a bar.

Wichita, in 1874, sported a population of 2,200. When Texas cowboys had gone home, the town's amatory needs were served by a mere five to seven local maidens who chose this method of augmenting the family purse. But with spring — as each cattle season approached — their numbers accelerated. During June through September, a total of about 50 cyprians plied their trades at Wichita.

In addition to its temperance laws, Kansas statutes labeled brothel-keeping and prostitution as misdemeanors. Mostly, these statutes were ignored in favor of a system of monthly fines that in practice amounted to indirect licenses to operate. Generally, the fines were modest, in the $5 to $8 range for each girl, with the amount doubled for the madame, plus $2 for court costs.

One of Wichita's most popular bartenders was "Rowdy Joe" Lower, a name derived from his method of contending with obstreperous customers. "Rowdy Kate," his wife, was allegedly able to out-shoot and drink more whisky than most of the town's men. Two of the five men she claimed to have shot were former husbands.

When cattle brought prosperity to Kansas, saloon-men in Dodge City formed their own vigilante committee to combat toughness. They were led by a man known as Fancy Pat. In one instance, they formed a posse, attacked the saloons, and left 14 men dead. One of the victims was riddled from head to foot. A local undertaker picked a number of common wood screws out of the body. Lots of people at that time used such hardware as ammunition for their shotguns to save the cost of buckshot.

Next morning the "regulators" employed carpenters to make seven large pine caskets. Two victims were put in each box and all were hauled to

AT RAWHIDE, NEVADA, The High Grade Bar, The
Northern and The Hermitage were all saloons. [Western
History Collection—Denver Public Library]

Boot Hill on two-horse wagons. Vigilantes joined the procession, each linking arms with a dancehall girl. Seven flasks of whisky were deposited in the graves, then the whole procession returned to Dodge City.

In the first year of its existence as a cattle town, Dodge City had 14 shootings. The first two men killed were blacks, soldiers from nearby Fort Dodge. No arrests were made. Dodge was divided by a 75-yard swath, running east to west, the railroad right-of-way. The Santa Fe Railroad tracks bounded the wide-open part of Dodge. Conveniently, the jail was there, too. North of the tracks was the respectable part of town, where cowboys were "discouraged." Guns were checked before crossing north of the tracks. A fine of $100 was assessed against violators.

Dodge City's vice district was also south of the railroad tracks. A long row of saloons, including "Chalk" Beeson's famed Long Branch, were available. And behind them, also in a row, stood the cribs, where dancehall girls, saloon lassies, and other practitioners of the world's oldest profession, plied their trade. When "Chalk" Beeson first took over the Long Branch Saloon, he hoped to make it a center of culture. He even put in a four-piece orchestra that played during peak hours in the main barroom.

Booming El Paso, Texas, sported 28 saloons by the 1870's. In Texas, trees were scarce and lumber was never plentiful. The railroad that reached El Paso brought red bricks, mahogany-finished bars, musical instruments and girls, all from the outside. Red-brick saloons became common and some even adopted that name.

San Antonio's most disreputable establishment was the notorious Vaudeville, a combination saloon and gambling house that stood near the Alamo. It was housed in a huge structure that also sported a theatre where scantily attired females hustled drinks and emoted their way through contrived dramatic episodes. At every opportunity,

ELDORA, COLORADO—a Boulder County gold camp—
was the location of the Arcade Saloon. [State Historical
Society of Colorado]

the girls did what they could to assure that the weight of silver dollars in the cowboys' pockets did not burden them on the way home. For the members of the audience who became sufficiently aroused by these academy-award performances, there were private rooms upstairs where the herders could meet the actresses under more congenial conditions. Locally, this row of cubicles was called Paradise Alley.

In Pottawatomie County, Texas, three saloon towns flourished in a six-mile area. They were called Youngs Crossing, Violet Springs and Corner. Violet Springs had 11 "booze bins." But Corner had more and was much wilder. Saloon shooting victims were dragged outside for 50 feet and deposited in the river. U.S. marshals left Corner alone for the first six years of its life. Corner's saloons were a refuge for horse thieves who used them to exchange stolen animals with persons coming from the opposite direction.

The term "bootlegger" may have started in these border saloons. Cowboys slipped flat bottles of liquor into their boot tops for smuggling into Indian Territory. Others tied jugs of whisky to their saddles and swam the river when it was swollen. All of these saloons violated the law by selling liquor to minors, to Indians and on Sundays.

Physicians were called to Corner's saloons several times each week to tend victims of knifings and shootings. Once there was a lawsuit over a saloon fight in which an ear was bitten off. In court, there were no witnesses who saw the biting, but several observed the biter spitting the ear out of his mouth.

The area got respectable after the turn of the century, and by 1903, Corner even had a post office. A flood in 1904 and prohibition in 1917 took a lot of steam out of Corner. In 1898, there were 62 saloons and 2 distilleries in Pottawatomie County. Only 14 of the original 27 towns now survive.

Many Western towns boasted saloons that were owned and sometimes operated by well-known or notorious persons. Ben Thompson, far-famed as a gunfighter, operated Thompson's Hall in Austin,

THIS RARE INTERIOR VIEW shows Dave Smith, owner, behind the bar of his saloon at Fort Robinson, Nebraska. [Western History Collection—Denver Public Library]

OBVERSE AND REVERSE of tokens from the P. Menapace Red Brick Saloon, Sopris, Colorado, and the Atlas Saloon, Columbus, Montana. [Collection of Robert L. Brown]

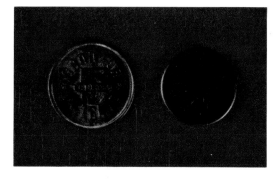

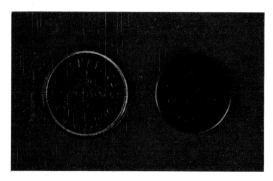

Texas, for a number of years. It was a rough place and something newsworthy could almost always be found there. Reporters considered it good copy. Thompson himself was a colorful character and hangers-on flocked around him like flies at a barbecue. His accounts of many thrilling adventures probably improved with each telling.

Once, when a pack of rowdy cowboys came to Austin to "see the elephant" and paint the place red, they thought Thompson's Hall would be a good place to start. Somehow, they mistook Thompson himself for a dude and started a systematic hazing with his new hat. He went along with the fun for the first couple of times, until they knocked it into the dirt. When guns appeared, the tables were turned. Thompson adroitly clipped the ear of one of his tormentors with a well-placed

A CODY, WYOMING, photographer staged this "typical" saloon picture. [Western History Collection—Denver Public Library]

shot. His identity established, the fun ended there.

Help for reformers occasionally came from unexpected quarters. When the citizens of Austin began to grow unhappy about their town's unsavory reputation, a reform movement was started. Saloon-owner Ben Thompson decided to add his two-bits when duly constituted authorities were unable to rout the gamier elements. Beginning in Thompson's Hall, his own saloon, he sent a few skillfully placed bullets into the bottled goods behind the bar, into the gaming tables, and topped the performance by scattering the neatly stacked columns of poker chips. His formidable reputation probably saved him when he entered the establishments of his competitors and administered more of the same treatment. As a finale, he completely cleaned out the red-light streets of Austin. But in 1880, Thompson's zealousness had subsided and

he opened up a new place. Most rowdy of all the saloons in Austin was the Senate. Whenever possible, the place was wide open and special holidays, including New Year's and Christmas, were celebrated by burlesque-like acts that featured nearly-nude saloon girls. Some sang, others danced, and all took part in risque dramatizations.

Western saloons in the cattle towns owed their popularity in large part to the fact that they were the only common meeting places for cowboys. Since they were not universally welcomed with open arms in the end-of-track cattle towns, cowboys became clannish. They met where they were welcome, and they spent their pay and did their celebrating in some of the worst saloons. However, the whole cowboy thing became obsolete and ceased to exist as a result of the Homestead Act and the invention of barbed wire.

THIS TURN-OF-THE-CENTURY saloon photograph was taken in Clovis, New Mexico. [State Historical Society of Colorado]

THE ORIGINAL LONG BRANCH Saloon on Dodge City's Front Street was photographed in 1876. [Kansas State Historical Society]

[Oil Painting by Jack Roberts]   [Ken Johnson Collection]

THE PROPOSITION

Chapter 8

SALOONS AND THE "LADIES" ————————————————————

FEW FAMILY-TYPE WOMEN ever saw the interior of a saloon prior to the Roaring Twenties. However, many ladies enjoyed a glass of schnapps now and then, and ways were devised to quench their thirsts. On stern-wheeled riverboats, there was usually a ladies' drinking lounge near the back end of one of the decks. Mostly, the ladies slipped-in when nobody was watching.

An incredible number of saloons had side doors leading to separate rooms equipped with horsehair sofas for the ladies. Some offered secluded private dining rooms that afforded protection from the raucous noises and sour athletic odors of the main barroom. In the few low-class bars where women could be legally served, there was often a separate entrance to a side room where drinks by the glass were available. Male waiters, not scantily-clad barmaids, brought drinks to the tables. Pretty landscapes and paintings of children at play, rather than traditional saloon art, hung on the walls. And gambling equipment was never found in these "ladies' ordinaries." Women in saloons resulted in hard days for the bartender, involving, in their words, "the appalling mess of mixed drinks." It was said that some of these concoctions resembled a canned-fruit salad drenched in whisky.

During their frequent anti-liquor crusades, militant feminists occupied stations outside of saloons to record who entered, how long he stayed, his condition upon departure, and if possible, how much and of what he had consumed on the premises. But at times, the tables were turned and the lookouts were males. Some Western towns made a game of feminine opposition to saloons. In the most common ploy, a lookout would be placed at one of the front windows to watch the sidewalk. Whenever a stern-visaged group of four or more women approached, the signal was given. Just as the ladies passed the swinging doors, the men

inside would give voice to a volley of the most repugnant barroom nouns, common profanity and indelicate expressions. And in junior high schools all across America, the same psychology is tried almost daily on deans of girls and first-year lady teachers, with almost boring frequency.

There were women of other persuasions who waited outside saloons, too, but for quite different purposes. When intoxicated males emerged, one or more of these women might approach and ask for a match, picking his pocket when he reached inside his coat.

Women were the saloons' most persistent opponents, partly because some of their husbands sought out saloons as a means of getting away from emasculation. European males maintain exclusive clubs for the same reason. Prohibition marked the zenith of a militant women's war against liquor dispensaries that took their husbands away from home in the evening.

Another favorite technique of anti-saloon feminists began with a public-indignation meeting. Prayers were offered, hymns and protest songs were rendered and fiery speeches were made. When a proper fever point had been attained, they would leave the hall in a body and march on the closest saloon. Chanting slogans about the demon rum, they would storm through the swinging doors and kneel in prayer on the barroom floor. Men who recognized wives and daughters escaped through the gambling room at the back. Meanwhile, the kneeling ladies exhorted the gents to join

them in prayer and hymns, and the men invited the ladies to join them in a glass of beer. There was little rapprochement between the opposing sides.

In one instance, a group of women tried to reform a saloon by stocking it with books and converting it into a library, but the errant boys avoided the place. Some of the more-sensitive sisters began to cross streets to avoid walking past a saloon. In this way they could avoid the rather theatrical Victorian practice of public fainting upon having heard an obscenity. Deliberately false stories were sometimes planted by bartenders with selected patrons who had the ear of the leading anti-saloon gabblers. The goal, to keep women out of the thirst parlors, was largely realized for many years.

As a form of protest against the antics of the unpredictable Carry Nation, saloons sometimes displayed large, framed mottos that read, "All Nations Welcome Except Carry." Tiny South Pass City, Wyoming, needed no outside reformers. It had its own built-in talent in the person of Esther Morris. Mrs. Morris' hat store, now empty, still stands in the town. Esther was a reformer, but she never interfered with the town's 13 saloons, nor its

DANCEHALL TOKENS like these sometimes were called dance "chits" or "checks." [Collection of Robert L. Brown]

infamous White Swan saloon and parlor house. Her thing was voting rights for women. Mrs. Morris was responsible for the pressure resulting in enactment of Wyoming's Woman Suffrage law on December 10, 1889 — America's first. How she allegedly used drinks and entertainment on reluctant legislators makes a wonderful, though impossible-to-check, story. South Pass City — alas — is a ghost town now, sitting forlornly atop the Continental Divide.

A woman quite different from Esther Morris was Martha "Calamity Jane" Canary, who was rarely permitted inside the saloons of Deadwood for fear she would give them a bad name. And yet, she had an enormous appetite for alcohol. She bought drinks from the side door "ladies entrances" of the Nugget, Happy Hour and Miners Delight. Martha often dressed as a man and was sometimes mistaken for one. What's more, her choice of language didn't help in identification of her gender. When intoxicated, she would assail male enemies, cursing them, their forbears and their offspring, calling them dogs and sons of those animals.

TWO VIEWS of the same 19th-Century "saloon girl." Why was one garter above the knee, while the other was below? [Collection of Freda and Francis Rizzari]

Because dancing was a favorite indoor sport on the frontier, larger saloons retained a bevy of dancehall girls. Lonesome trappers, miners, cowboys or loggers could buy a ticket and dance around the room a few times. Prices ranged from 5 cents to $1, and the girl split her "take" with the proprietor. Afterwards, the man was expected to buy her a drink at the bar. And for a price, other ancillary services were available. Most dances were short, seldom more than three minutes, "to allow the musicians a rest." And some of these ladies were not above picking the pockets of an intoxicated partner.

The much-mentioned leveling influence prevalent in frontier saloons was also extended to the women who were employed there as barmaids or entertainers. No sources have been found to indicate that they were ever treated as inferiors. The startling fact that many men, not just a few, married these women is revealing. Possibly their status as servants deterred barmaids from interfering with gambling and male arguments, making them seem submissive and more acceptable to men who frequented these places.

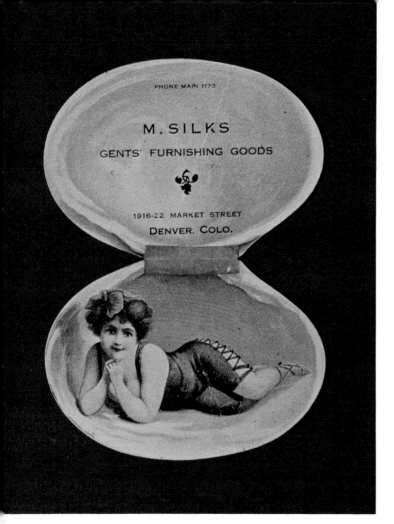

MADAM MATTIE SILKS, proprietress of Denver's most opulent parlor houses, used this folding oyster-shell card to advertise her establishment on Market Street. [Collection of Jim Wright]

IT PAYS TO ADVERTISE! A saloon advertisement from the 1903 Leadville business directory. Notice the last entry. [Collection of George Casey]

Although women were banned by law or custom from a majority of America's saloons, Volunteers of America or Salvation Army lassies were welcomed. While feminists were greeted with a barrage of profanity, all improper language ceased when the above-named ladies in uniform entered the swinging doors. Men who forgot their manners invited a "knuckle sandwich." The respect accorded these women often included being offered a seat and a meal from the free lunch. But in Victorian America, they were never offered a drink.

Where ladies were not permitted, children were likewise banned for their own good. And yet, in 19th-Century America, it was the youngsters who were the message-carriers and errand-runners for parents and other adults, the means by which small chores were done, and the kids got pocket money in the process. So, methods had to be contrived to get around legal obstacles surrounding that most common of errands, sending a youngster down to the corner for a bucket of suds. Since children were not allowed inside saloons, the

IN LEADVILLE the Union Pacific Saloon and the St. Louis House— with girls in the upstairs windows— could be found in the rowdy district. [Collection of David S. Digerness]

common practice involved sending 10 cents and an empty lard pail with the child. A loud yell directed under the swinging "bat-wing" doors brought someone to fill the bucket, while the lad stayed legally outside. Then, a fast run back home was necessary before the head of suds receded.

In Reno, during the early part of the present century, enterprising young boys were able to augment their allowances with a minor variation of the common old routine of beer delivered by the pail. At the noon lunch break, groups of youngsters would appear at construction sites throughout the city. Each boy carried a long shovel or rake handle equipped with six or eight brass hooks and a like number of empty lard pails. Orders were taken and the boys raced off to the closest saloon. Moments later they were back with buckets of freshly drawn tap beer to wash down the workmen's lunches.

Some laborers supplied their own containers. The five-pound lard pail was the most popular. A subtle but continual war developed between thirsty customers and saloonkeepers. Before handing the pail and the dime to the boy, workmen would dip an index finger into the lard, butter from a sandwich, or grease from the job, and smear a ring around the inside of the pail, just beneath the top of the pail's rim. This practical ritual tended to retard the formation of foam heads, thus assuring more beer and less suds in their pails. Bartenders, in the face of dwindling profit margins and managerial exhortations, would furtively wipe the insides of each pail with a bar towel, hopefully discouraging the customer's greed for a more favorable beer-suds ratio. Neither side ever aired their grievance openly in the presence of the enemy, but the undeclared, undercover hassle continued for years.

In addition to the rowdy skid-row types of saloons, there were also a number of quiet, family types of places. Only their names were competitively similar. Many had a European aura. Where permitted by law, whole families frequented them, and mother could enjoy a schooner of schnapps

with her household.

But not all of the ladies who were found around saloons were side-door customers, family types, or reformers. Some were there to practice the world's most ancient professional service. Behind the larger saloons stood a disorderly row of shabbily constructed shacks, usually unpainted, of rough-pine siding with one or two partitions and a Dutch door for each room that fronted on an alley. These were the cribs, and the whole architectural array was known in most towns as "the row." Bret Harte called it by a different name. When such a facility was attached to a saloon, he referred to it as the "unspeakable annex."

During peak business hours, the crib girls opened the tops of their doors, leaning on the bottom sections, wearing smiles but little else. On some of the higher class "rows," the girl's name and sometimes her financial quotation was posted on the door. The names, of course, were fictitious but mostly they were suggestive of this occupation. Dawson City had its Golden Gut Gertie and Diamond Dust Lil. Names like Klondike Katy or Musterole Maggie and Madame Comstock were common in other camps. For the man unfortunate enough to become thirsty in such places, beer sold

for a dollar a bottle. Venereal diseases were common. Without Penicillin, men waited for them to go away, enduring them like the common cold.

Very few Kansas cowtown saloons used barmaids. Burly men seemed better able to cope with unruly cowboys. But now and then, prostitutes were given soliciting privileges. If a saloon maintained a string of girls, most of them fitted into one of two categories. The first catered to the needs of the town's wealthy establishment. The others, older and less easy on the eyes, worked the Texas cowboy trade. An unofficial survey estimated that some 50 prostitutes worked in Wichita in 1874, the last big year for cattle drives. In some Kansas cowtowns, portable brothels, called "cat wagons," arrived with the cattle drives and were parked in back of the saloons.

As a means of self-protection, many married couples supported dancehalls, saloons and redlight areas. One fine lady who had lived through most of the Cripple Creek era told the writer that most families never even locked their doors while Myers Avenue was "open" and operating. Potential troublemakers congregated there and left the rest of the city in peace. The feeling among Cripple Creek's pioneers was that such places were a deterrent to crime. Since both classes of crime and frequency of crime statistics are so incomplete and so subject to interpretation, objective research in these areas is most difficult. Young, vigorous, single males abounded on the frontier. The tradition of respect for married women and their daughters was very prevalent in the West. The existence of and obvious comparisons between family-type women and the other variety tended to widen the gulf and to enhance the tradition.

Few meaningful generalizations can be drawn about the role of women in relation to saloons. For wherever there was a rule of exclusion rooted in tradition or the law, there were also those who sought and found ways to circumvent it. For while women certainly influenced the sociology of the saloon, practices were by no means uniform or consistent across the American West.

CELESTE FATTOR'S infamous Tremount saloon and brothel stood on Silverton's Blair Street from 1908 until 1915. [Collection of Richard A. Ronzio]

Silverton. Colo. April 23ᵗʰ 189 1900

Mess Chiono & Giacomalli

Bought of

SAN JUAN BOTTLING WORKS,
GEO. NOLL & CO., Props.,
...BOTTLERS OF...
WM. J. LEMP BREWING CO'S
ST. LOUIS LAGER BEER.

[Collection of Fritz Klinke]

[Oil Painting by Jack Roberts] [Ken Johnson Collection]

CAN CAN

Chapter 9

CRIME AND THE SALOON

AN UNUSUALLY LARGE NUMBER of crimes — some quite serious — happened in saloons and gambling halls. On March 11, 1884, Ben Thompson and King Fisher, both notorious gunmen, were shot in San Antonio's Vaudeville Theatre. The Vaudeville was a variety den and saloon. The shows on its stage were earthy and contrived, performed by scantily clad ladies. Following the show, the performers were available for other kinds of entertainment in the less-public rooms upstairs. The Vaudeville fronted on San Antonio's main plaza, not far from the historic old Alamo Mission.

John Selman and John Wesley Hardin, both gunslingers, were the principals in a shooting at the Acme Saloon in El Paso on August 19, 1895. Actually, a fight had been expected, but Selman shot Hardin in the back of the head while the latter rolled dice on the end of the bar.

Just a few months later, on April 5, 1896, Selman shot it out with George Scarborough in El Paso's Wigwam saloon. The actual shooting, being bad for business, was done in the alley at the rear of the building. Four shots were fired, patrons inside insisted that the building shook, and those who rushed out into the alley found Selman sprawled in the dirt. The investigating U.S. deputy marshal called it "a gentlemen's duel," but a search of the body revealed no pistol. Scarborough had fired all of the shots.

Sometimes, saloons were used as a deliberate front for crimes. Jeff's Place in Skagway, Alaska, was one such example. Its proprietor was Jefferson Randolph "Soapy" Smith, an excessively dishonest con-man from Georgia, Colorado and other points. Smith is most vividly remembered at a safe downwind distance from history. During his Colorado years he was active in Denver, Cripple Creek and Creede. His work crew included short-card artists, thimbleriggers, and shell men who regularly accompanied him to new towns when things got too hot.

Soapy's saloon and skinning house at Creede was called the Orleans Club. Other con-artists who tried to operate there were forced to hand over half of their profits to Smith. Once, after a shooting at the Orleans, one of the trusted employees pushed his way through the crowd. He knelt beside the body, sobbing out remorse for his true friend. Suddenly, he clasped the corpse to him and pressed his face to the chest of the departed. At the same time he carefully bit off the $2,500 diamond stud from the victim's shirt.

During the Spanish-American War, Smith set up a fake Army recruiting station where pockets were picked while the men took physical exams. Several cities, like Denver, ran him out. But soon after his arrival in Alaska, he organized a takeover and soon ruled Skagway.

He set up a telegraph office, but all of the messages were funneled through Jeff's Place to determine how much gold the sender had. Other members of Soapy's crowd steered victims to the saloon on the basis of how prosperous they might be, judged by the appearance of their luggage.

The area behind the saloon served as a urinal, and Smith also kept an eagle chained to a perch out there. Among informed segments of Skagway's population, "seeing the eagle" meant being slugged and robbed by alley thugs on Smith's payroll.

When Skagway got tired of its bad reputation, a vigilante committee, calling itself the Committee of

THE INFAMOUS "SOAPY" SMITH—standing at center
—was photographed in his saloon in Skagway, Alaska.
[Western History Collection—Denver Public Library]

One-Hundred and One, was formed to get rid of Soapy and his gang. When Smith tried to infiltrate the law-and-order group's meeting, there was a shoot-out in the street outside. Frank Reid, the planner who drew the Skagway town plat, was the other antagonist. Both men shot and both were killed. Although Frank Reid is forgotten, there is now a reconstructed Jeff's Place in Skagway, where dudes from the "lower 48" can belly up to the bar and rest their sneakers on the brass rail, while mumbling brave, alcoholic platitudes.

By 1885, 6,000 miners and camp-followers crowded into Tin Cup, Colorado. Until vigilante action changed the town's complexion, the rowdy element held control of city officials, and Tin Cup's history reflects this misfortune. Allegedly, the first seven sheriffs were murdered in the first few months of the community's life. The lawless cemetery, or "boot hill marble orchard," contains more burials than the combined Protestant and Catholic plots.

Although it was never a big place, Tin Cup had a couple of typical saloons. Sim La Plant & Company operated the slightly more sedate of the two. And then there was the establishment of Arthur N. Perault & Company, commonly called Frenchy's Place. Frenchy Perault had the best-looking girls in town. Note in the accompanying photograph that his whole operation was housed in a two-story building. His saloon and various gambling equipment occupied only the lower floor, leaving the upstairs rooms for his other enterprises. Miners and freighters from all over Taylor Park migrated to Tin Cup to spend their weekends and paychecks. Tin Cup never did get around to building a church. It just was not that kind of a town.

The quality of the bottled goods sold in frontier saloons was probably reflected in the frequent fights and shootings. Instead of dispensing first-class liquor, greedy bartenders often stretched their profits by adding fusel oil, tobacco, water, red

THIS WAS BOB FORD'S saloon in Creede, Colorado, during 1896. [Collection of Freda and Francis Rizzari]

pepper, lye or whatever was handy.

The potency of some saloon-dispensed firewaters can only be evaluated in light of the behavior of their customers. "General" Jack Smith once got enchantingly stewed in Dingman's saloon in Victor, Colorado. Within the hour, he launched a one-man attack on the town of Altman, in the course of which he freed all of the prisoners in the Altman jail. Later, after he had sobered up, he was arrested in Victor by order of Marshal Kelly of Altman. However, when Smith was let out on bail, he made a beeline for the Gavin & Toohey saloon, where he waited for Kelly, precipitated a pretty traditional shoot-out and was killed. Perhaps another seige at Dingman's whisky vats might have produced a different result.

Because of the risk of damage to the bottled stock, shoot-outs were discouraged inside of saloons. Whenever arguments reached a fever pitch,

the antagonists were asked to settle it outside. However, sometimes the amenities were not observed. Jim and Bat Masterson killed the bartender of Dodge City's Lady Gay saloon on the premises. The hastily convened jury understood about such things and fined the brothers a mere $10.

In far too many instances, the distinction between bawdyhouses, dancehalls and saloons was almost non-existent. Nearly all dancehalls were saloons, and far too many were little more than fronts for prostitution.

In Wyoming, when located near military posts, saloons and dancehalls of this type were often called "hog ranches." During the Indian wars, hog ranches could be found near several of the biggest Western military installations. Whisky, gambling and saloon girls were offered. Some soldiers called them soiled angels, while others preferred the more

ANIMAL HEADS, saloon art and gambling equipment adorned the backroom of the Pioneer Saloon in Leadville, **Colorado.** [Western History Collection—Denver Public Library]

earthy designations. Confidence men, gamblers and road agents found homes away from home at the hog ranches. Each location sported its own little cemetery, where the less-fortunate customers were interred.

Incidentally, hog ranches had no connection with pigs. The name was probably coined to describe the behavior of those persons who frequented the premises. In one version, it was said that the name described how each of the women had a following of soldiers who looked like the solemn procession of a sow with several little pigs.

Since Fort Laramie was adjacent to the Oregon Trail, there were a number of hog ranches in its neighborhood. The infamous 6-Mile Ranch stood at about that distance southwest of the fort. Soldiers gambled, acquired social diseases, and got drunk on its premises. Military attire was the uniform of the day for female employees, thus

making it easier to smuggle such persons into barracks at the fort. Since it cut down their income from liquor and gambling, hog-ranch owners took a dim view of such liaisons. Only a few foundations along 6-Mile Creek still mark the site. Beyond it, on the hillside above the creek, are the mounded graves of six victims who died there.

At the 6-Mile Ranch, the bedding was aired once each week. Airing consisted of spreading the blankets out on the ground for the day. The preferred place was on the top of a huge nest of red ants. Body lice, much too common in 19th-Century America, were dispatched and eaten by the ants. Lice were brought regularly from the fort by troopers on their nocturnal visits.

The 3-Mile Hog Ranch was started in 1872, and it was only three miles southwest of Fort Laramie, just east of the Laramie River. Later, it was moved across the river. Their first building was a log

FRENCHY PERRAULT, proprietor of Frenchy's Place in Tin Cup, Colorado, was holding the horse at right. The inset shows tokens used here. [Collection of Freda and Francis Rizzari]

OBVERSE AND REVERSE of a token from the Office Bar, Bisbee, Arizona, and one from the New State Bar, Silver City, New Mexico. [Collection of Richard A. Ronzio]

structure about 45 feet square. It still had rifle ports in the walls that dated back to Indian-fighting days. The imaginative skill of military peeping toms dictated its abandonment.

Just east of the log fortress, a cluster of rude structures housed a bunkhouse, store, warehouse, icehouse, blacksmith shop and the inevitable saloon. A low-roofed structure of grout construction housed the main attraction. Once, during a slack period when business fell off, a dozen or so new sporting women were imported from Omaha, Kansas City and Denver. Eight new double-room duplexes were put up to accommodate them.

Among this motley female crew was one Martha "Calamity Jane" Canary, an excessively soiled practitioner who made this her home between military expeditions — which she accompanied in male attire. Abandoned prior to 1890, 3-Mile House left only four lonely graves to mark its site.

THIS COMBINATION HOTEL and Saloon stood on Ohio Pass in 1882. [Collection of Gary Christopher]

In Virginia City, Montana, at the Smith & Boyd Saloon, the bar was never fastened down to the puncheon floor. Drunks and pranksters would stand at the ends, lifting it off the floor just enough to rattle and bounce the glasses and bottles of startled and slightly tipsy customers.

It was widely believed that the quality — or lack of it — in a whisky determined the morals and mental state of the intoxicated. For example, Barney Hughes of Virginia City, Montana, speculated that bad liquor had made George Ives an outlaw. "A load of Virginia City whisky," he declared, "would lead a man to rob a crucified savior." Such pronouncements, of course, gained wide credence in saloons and were probably improved with each telling.

Some types of crime often associated with public drinking places were in reality quite uncommon. For example, saloon holdups, like Indian attacks on organized towns, were rare outside of badly researched movies or pulp fiction. There were a few of each, but not many because of the obviously bad odds and too many witnesses. One well-documented saloon holdup did occur at Fort Sumner, New Mexico, but most barroom crimes were far less theatrical.

Much early law enforcement and no little local government was transacted inside the saloons of frontier towns across the American West. Judge Roy Bean, the eccentric so-called "Law West of the Pecos," convened his court in a saloon. But the traditional portrait of George Washington never hung above the bench in Bean's courtroom. The Judge admired Lily Langtry, a popular entertainer of the day from New Jersey, who was short on morals but long on pulchritude. Miscreants unfortunate enough to be tried in Bean's saloon could view Lily's likeness during the trial, while hammers and saws were heard erecting the gallows outside.

Pioneer Denver had its share of saloon crime. In 1860, at the old Louisiana Saloon, James A. Gordon picked out John Gantz as his victim, threw him on the floor and placed a pistol at his temple. Gordon resented the influx of foreign-born miners, and proclaimed loudly that the mines of the territory were for Americans only. Gantz offered no resistance, and Gordon shot him while the pub-crawlers voiced their displeasure. Gordon escaped to Fort Lupton, then to Coffey County, Kansas. Sheriff William Middaugh tracked him there and

AT TURRET, COLORADO, Bob's Place at the extreme left in this view was the local saloon. Note the "ladies" on the balcony of the Golden Wonder Hotel. [State Historical Society of Colorado]

returned him to Denver, where a miners' court sentenced him to be hanged. Sheriff Middaugh, who also functioned as hangman, by tradition then set up drinks for all in the Louisiana Saloon. Miners removed their hats in honor of Gantz, whose blood still stained the rough-plank floor.

The most famous saloon killing of all time was probably that of James Butler (Wild Bill) Hickok. The date was August 1, 1876, and the place was the Mann & Lewis Saloon in Deadwood, South Dakota. Since Hickok held all aces and eights when shot, this combination is still called a "dead man's hand." Hickok sat calmly playing poker with his back not to the wall, as he usually preferred, but toward the door. Cross-eyed Jack McCall entered the building from the rear during betting on a hand. With just three feet separating his revolver and the victim, he shot Hickok through the head. When queried about why he shot from behind, McCall answered that he did not

want to commit suicide. A saloon as the crime's locale was incidental. Actually, Hickok made his headquarters in a local bordello.

In some cases, criminal gangs met in saloons because, as with their law-abiding contemporaries, it afforded the only place to meet and plan. In their case, the results were crimes and robberies of one sort or another. In pioneer San Francisco there were 1,200 murders during the town's first two years of life. Another source claims 1,000 homicides between 1849 and 1856 — either figure is alarming.

Crime and the misuse of liquor in America are still coupled with disastrous results. Our most recent national crime statistics state that liquor is a factor in at least one-third of our serious crimes. While this does not mean that all who use liquor must become criminals, it does indicate that many would-be crooks still bolster up their courage with alcohol.

113

[Oil Painting by Jack Roberts]

THE ENTERTAINERS

Chapter 10
MUSIC AND PREACHING IN THE SALOON ————————————————

MUCH OF THE TRADITIONAL FOLK MUSIC associated with the early West is about as Western as New York City. Like the cowboy and the saloon, it was by no means a uniquely American product of the frontier. And yet, a great deal of music was performed in saloons, particularly in the cattle towns, during the late 1860's and through the 1870's. Lots of tuneful old refrains came from the South, the East, or from Europe. Many of them were protest songs of that time, openly critical of the Eastern establishment, its lifestyle and attitude toward the Westerner.

One of the most popular songs was *Streets of Laredo*. Our Western version of this refrain was lifted from a 16th Century London street ditty that detailed the regrets of a young lover dying of syphilis. *The Cowboy's Dream* borrows the melody of the folk song *My Bonnie Lies Over the Ocean*. George Custer's 7th Cavalry rode into battle to the sprightly strains of *Garry Owen*, which was openly kited from an old bromide known as the *Irish Washerwoman*. The ever-popular *Red River Valley* came from an 18th-Century melody that was first sung in upstate New York as *The Bright Mohawk Valley*.

The many verses of *Sweet Betsy From Pike* were composed in Virginia City, Montana, to ridicule prospectors from Pike County, Missouri. Of the more than 225 known verses, at least 200 of them are obscene. The original tune, by the way, was kited from a street melody that was first popular in William Shakespeare's time. Even today, popular songs appear to have been lifted from Peter Tchaikovsky, and Georg Philipp Telemann, among others. And so it goes.

One of the objectionable features noted by non-saloon crowds was the loud singing that emanated from the swinging doors. Most of the preferred melodies were choral. Among favored themes were laments for Mother, personal loneliness, the virtues of a fairly wide assortment of lost causes, and the temptations heaped upon poor working girls. *The Drunkards Doom*, a much-

rendered old throat clutcher of the Anti-Saloon League, was another favorite that was always belted out with great enthusiasm and feeling by bar patrons.

Most saloons provided music of some sort. If an orchestra, piano player, or vocalist was beyond their means, there was always a music box. When a saloon had a band, it probably tootled popular melodies of the day like *Zizzy, Ze, Zum, Zum*, or *Sugar Baby*. Many orchestral groups were retained on a part-time basis, with Saturday nights being the most in demand. A part of their income came from passing the hat several times each evening.

Many of the larger-and-more-prosperous saloons hired orchestral musicians on a regular schedule. Vocalists were employed on the same basis. Poorer saloons got along with honky-tonk pianos, a fiddle or an accordion, commonly called the "stomach Steinway." Vocal musicians were recruited from among the customers and were rewarded by having coins thrown if their efforts pleased the crowd. Sometimes the hat was passed and the owner kept a percentage of the take. The influence of saloons on popular dance crazes cannot be overlooked. *The Turkey Trot* and *Bunny Hug*, among others, trace their origins to such places.

New Orleans collected a $100 fee from saloons that offered instrumental music. The fee was doubled if vocalists performed. The vocal repertoire included several old tear-jerkers like *Aunt Clara, Hang on the Bell Nellie, My Wild Irish Rose*

IN 1910, THE COSMOPOLITAN Saloon in Telluride, Colorado, sported this orchestra "for culture." [Western History Collection—Denver Public Library]

and *Oh Where is My Wandering Boy Tonight?* If stage shows were offered, the city fathers of New Orleans skimmed $300 off the top.

In pioneer towns, there was no lodge, corner drugstore or club. There was little reading matter and few of the men were literate anyway. There were almost no schoolhouses and few churches. Consequently, even clergymen used the saloons — as gathering places. Pioneer towns across the West had many saloons and gambling halls, but few churches. Lacking more conventional houses of worship, many men of the cloth preached in saloons. Rev. John L. (Father) Dyer said that he was always treated with courtesy in such places. Actually, few community facilities could hold as many bodies as the local barroom.

The bar itself became the altar, most "professors" could dash off a few hymns on the honky-tonk piano, and thirsty congregations usually bought lots of whisky after the services. To get things started, saloon owners were known to have donated money to "the reverend." Barroom art was often draped during the services. Bartenders were always pleased to see a parson coming. An hour of preaching left behind a multitude of parched throats that felt the need of some communion wine — or whatever.

In Cripple Creek, the first Sunday-school service was held in the Buckhorn Saloon. Mother Duffy — the well-known faro dealer whose trombone-voiced vocabulary would have shamed a sea captain — owned the place. At the appointed time on a Sunday morning, she ordered all of her "girls" from the Buckhorn's upstairs rooms to dress up in their best and come down to the bar. There they sat during the lesson. When a drunk demanded service and got noisy about it, muscular Mother Duffy dispatched him by a unique combination of brute force and appropriately colorful verbiage, with an occasional word from the scriptures. After assigning his soul to perdition, she threw him bodily across the board sidewalk into a row of horses tied up to the Buckhorn's rail. Then, the Sunday school continued.

When revivalist clergymen stepped off the coach from the East, the local saloon was often their first stop, where arrangements for prayer meetings were concluded. Only a few brought their own revival-meeting-sized tents; most lacked such financial backing and used the dram parlors.

At the Close & Patterson Saloon in Las Vegas, New Mexico, religious services were a regular feature. Life-size girlie pictures were covered and the bar was draped. One day a pair of itinerant preachers entered and asked permission to hold services. A bevy of lady missionaries followed them inside. They sang, preached and exhorted at great length, describing the salient features of Hades with great realism. At the end, they were able to baptize four gamblers and 15 bar girls who were escorted to the draped bar altar by two hard cases named Lazy Liz and Nervous Jessie.

The Reverend Thomas Uzzell, who erected the first church in Leadville, Colorado, often preached in saloons, brawling with the men to gain respect. In fact, the Reverend Uzzell first saw the light in such a place when he attended a revival. His original reason for going involved a plan to shoot peas from upstairs at the worshipers while they were busy with prayer.

For unknown reasons, many Western saloons were operated by former preachers. This curious,

THE REV. JOHN L. "FATHER" DYER, early Methodist circuit rider, often preached in saloons. [Western History Collection—Denver Public Library]

SAN FRANCISCO'S EL DORADO saloon orchestra performed from an elevated platform along the back wall. [Western History Collection—Denver Public Library]

paradoxical relationship between the clergy and the grog shops has been the basis of much Western folklore and some legitimate history. An ex-preacher turned saloonkeeper at Nevada City, Montana, offered the use of his saloon for preaching purposes any time except Sundays. Sabbath breaking was common, and the place was just too busy.

In early America, when a new preacher was ordained, the investiture was sometimes held in a saloon. A special brew, called ordination beer, was reserved for such occasions. Union City, Montana — not far from wide-open Virginia City in Alder Gulch — was a temperance town. It not only had no saloons, but the town's gold mill was never allowed to run on Sundays.

If churches, rather than saloons, had seized the opportunity to provide leisure-time activities, one may only speculate on how different Western history might have been.

Chapter 11

SALOON TOKENS AND BAR BOTTLES ————————————————————————————————

IN A HISTORICAL SENSE, the use of token coinage goes far back into antiquity. Long before there was an American West, fractional coinage was an accepted medium of exchange. In nearly all cases, tokens came into use because of some shortage of small denomination coins that are so needed for making change. True to its definition, the token was indicative of something else. In this case, hard-money tokens were pieces of metal, symbolic of currency, having a face value greater than their actual or intrinsic value. They represented a currency no government would honor and no bank would redeem, but they were issued widely and redeemed by saloons. They were also called merchants' money, hard-times tokens, merchants' tokens, seco, trade checks or trade tokens.

Some were valued at a mere penny. Most were distinctly fractional in nature. The 12½-cent token was a very widely used fraction in saloons. Others were issued with 5-, 10-, 25-, 30-, 50-, 60- or 75-cent designations on their reverse sides. Earliest of all the fractional tokens from the saloon era were for a mere 2½ cents.

In the West, the mining period brought about conditions that perpetuated the already prevailing scarcity of hard money. From the time of the first gold discoveries in 1849, one may trace Western saloon history through the gold and silver camps by means of privately minted currency. Following the Civil War, adventure-seekers from nearly every state in the Union migrated into the mining towns in search of quick wealth. With increased numbers of people in the Western territories, the already-insufficient supply of legal money grew even shorter. In the face of this condition — coupled with a lack of stability of the money already in circulation — Western merchants began to issue trade coins of their own to fill the gap. Sometimes, saloons accepted other trader's tokens, saving them up until they had a quantity large enough to be redeemed at the establishment of their competitor.

"Merchants' money"— as it was sometimes called — was used by a rather wide variety of commercial enterprises, aside from saloons. The list of such firms included livery stables, card rooms, lumber camps, restaurants, cigar stores, billiard rooms, public dancehalls and poolhalls that used tokens as payoffs for winning games. Also included were amusement parks, trading posts, sutlers, dairies, military posts, prisons, cattle companies, company-owned mining camps, individual mines, schools, toll bridges and toll roads. Some other businesses that used merchants' tokens were electric transit companies, mills, refineries (which used them to keep track of the number of wagonloads of concentrates hauled) and general stores (where they were used to extend credit). And many times, there also was a saloon on the premises as a sideline for at least half of the preceding businesses.

Saloons most commonly used a variety of token known as the "bar chit," "beer chip" or "check for a short beer." Along with the name of the saloon, they bore such messages as, "Good for a glass of beer," "Good for 5 cents at the bar." "Good for one shot of Red Eye," or some other invitation to partake of an appropriate libation. When the economy grew prosperous in the late 1870's, the price of beer went up from 5 cents to 10 cents, then to 25 cents for two glasses. As a consequence, a new colloquial expression appeared in our language.

When miners, cattlemen and others entered a saloon, it was common practice to put down 25

THIS IS THE CRYSTAL BAR at Virginia City, Nevada.
Note the bar-bottle display. [Collection of Robert L.
Brown]

cents for two beers. Since the beer schooners were
large, the customer was sometimes unable to drink
more than one. And how does a bartender refund
12½ cents in change? To resolve this quandary, the
12½-cent token, or "check for a short beer,"
appeared and was instantly accepted. Thus began
one of the unique types of token currency. In some
quarters the short-beer check was known as a
"bit" token, and the term "two bits" became a
popular synonym for 25-cent pieces, and has survived to this day. Within the trade, saloon tokens
had many uses. One collector insists that the
12½-cent variety was used only for whisky and that
the 5-cent type was used as a house-issued pass to
keep the bums away from the free lunches — described elsewhere — that were a standard fixture in
most saloons. A shot of whisky cost 15 cents or two
drinks for 25 cents. The 12½-cent checks un-
doubtedly were also used for whisky. Actually,
there was little uniformity of practice, each
saloonkeeper made his own rules to suit the
demands of his business.

Jack Slade, the awful-tempered highwayman
who murdered Jules Beni (or Remi) — among
others — had his own saloon tokens for use when
he had no money. Three different versions of

Slade's treatment of old Jules exist, including one
by Mark Twain. But in all of them, Jack cut off
Jules' ears and carried them as pocket talismens. In
Virginia City's saloons, when the outlaw lacked
money or tokens, he simply placed Beni's dried-up
ears on the top of the bar. Terrified bartenders,
who had been regaled with too many stories of
Slade's drunken sadism, always accepted the ears
as legal tender. But, apparently, no saloonkeeper
ever put them in the cash drawer since they were
still in Slade's pocket when the vigilantes hanged
him.

Slade's offenses against good taste consisted of
riding his horse through saloons while he was
intoxicated, shooting his gun and destroying
gaming equipment, fighting, and non-payment of
his saloon bills. In a saloon-theatre he once yelled
profanities and made lewd suggestions to the
"actresses." Then, he stomped up and down the
streets rendering off-color songs that detailed
alleged indelicate relationships between local prostitutes and vigilante leaders. After destroying a
milk wagon, he was ordered to leave town. He both
defied and defiled the summons after tearing it up.
Of the story that the "local uplift" society dropped
him from the scaffold, or the local hanging tree,

there are two conflicting reports. But the saloon escapades of Jack Slade ended at Virginia City, and no other such tokens were ever known to have been used.

The Mormons of Utah and Colorado have always been a particularly hard-working, thrifty and self-sufficient people. Only a few saloon tokens were issued in Utah towns. More than most other groups, they have long cast a jaundiced eye at the American welfare system, and they used tokens to combat a common abuse. When assistance was necessary, the Latter Day Saints issued clearly marked tokens instead of money, thus assuring that the recipient would buy only at the Mormon store and that the "dole" would not be redeemed in the hated saloons for liquor or tobacco. Most Utah saloons were owned and operated by non-Mormons.

And if the redeemable purposes of bar tokens were unusual, their shapes and materials were even more diverse. Although round tokens were most common, there were also ovals, oblong shapes and doughnut-like varieties with a little hole cut out of the center. Hexagonal, diamond, octagonal, triangular, rectangular, heart and square shapes were also common. Somewhat less familiar types were sunburst, keystone, shield, deckled, sunflowered, star, cross, bell and petal shapes. A few were downright bizarre with a rounded-off square and four protruding points being employed in the same piece. The Ajax Saloon in Victor, Colorado, issued such a token.

Materials from which tokens were fabricated included wood, pot metal, copper, plastic, nickel, fibre, brass, aluminum, composition, zinc, German or Mexican silver, silver-nickel alloys, tin, white metals, bronze and lead. A somewhat rarer type was the bi-metal token, in which two different metals were combined in a single coin. The one shown in the accompanying photograph has a brass outer ring, with a center of aluminum. Tokens of this type are particularly prized by the collector.

Physically, most tokens bear the name and often the address of the issuer on one side. Usually, the city and state are included as well. On the reverse side, the value and purpose appear. Those tokens that lack complete information are called "mavericks" and are much less desirable to the collector than are those that tell a complete story.

Saloon tokens were the trading stamps of their day. Not only were they used as trade coins, they also functioned as captive advertising media, for identification, as convenience money in making change, for credit, as gifts, for discount purposes, as souvenirs, house checks, patriotic items, to help

THE CHICAGO SALOON of Silverton, Colorado, was in business on Greene Street from 1899 until 1908. The building still stands, but no longer serves as a saloon. [Collection of Richard A. Ronzio]

stimulate trade, or in other cases, to restrict trade. They were an illegal necessity coinage; the pocket money or small change of their day.

Officially, the government in Washington never approved of saloon tokens. From time to time, a maze of conflicting regulations emerged from the Treasury Department. Most of them were openly ignored. In the West, there were too few enforcement officers. They were severely overworked and their problems were of a far more serious nature. During the 1860's the government was preoccupied with the Civil War and was not overly concerned with media of exchange.

In the decades following the turn of the century, the number of token coins in circulation accelerated rapidly, reaching a peak in the 1930's. A few are still in use today; but the practice is largely a thing of the past, possibly because we no longer suffer from a coin shortage, and the need for small-change tokens has thus disappeared. Also, the price of a drink — any drink — has gone far

beyond 12½ cents. Some transportation lines still use tokens, a few restricted-parking facilities find them useful; and now and again, a business firm issues a batch to advertise its wares. But in most cases, the tokens of today are an anachronism, somewhat out of place in the fast-paced computer-mangled world of today. And yet, they also serve as a reminder of a colorful-and-interesting phase of economic and social life in the saloons of the American West.

AT UPPER LEFT we see a front view of a token offered by the Steve Jelbert Saloon, Nevadaville, Colorado, and the Brooks & Duran Saloon, Sherrod, Colorado. [Collection of Jim Wright]

FRONT VIEW only of tokens from the Hoffman Saloon, Colorado City, and the Dalsout & Cerolini Saloon, Central City, Colorado. [Collection of Robert L. Brown]

BOTH SIDES of tokens from John O'Leary's Daisy Saloon, Leadville, Colorado. [Collection of Robert L. Brown]

OBVERSE AND REVERSE sides of tokens from the Home Ranch Saloon, Cheyenne, Wyoming, and the Metropole Saloon, Rico, Colorado. [Collection of Robert L. Brown]

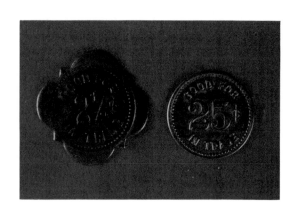

AT UPPER LEFT is a front only view of tokens from the Farmers' Exchange Saloon, La Jara, Colorado, and from the Haden Saloon. [Collection of Jim Wright]

FRONT VIEW ONLY of tokens from the Newport Saloon, Cripple Creek, Colorado, and Alfred Sam's Alamo Saloon, Animas Forks, Colorado. [Collection of Jim Wright]

RARE 6¼-CENT TOKEN from the Manhattan Bar, Park City, Utah, and a 1½-cent token from the Chicago Saloon, Silverton, Colorado. [Collection of Robert L. Brown]

FRONT VIEW ONLY of tokens from the Fred Bertoldi Saloon, Freeland, Colorado, and James Delaney's Turf Saloon, Como, Colorado. [Collections of Jim Wright and Ed Haley]

OBVERSE AND REVERSE sides of tokens from the Bimetallic Exchange Saloon, Creede, Colorado and Murphy's Saloon, Victor, Colorado. [Collection of Robert L. Brown]

123

FROM LEFT, an old beer stein with thumb tab on handle, a Tiffany Club brandy, a decorated whisky flask, a Bouvier's Buchu Gin, a three-piece round and a square whisky. [Collection of Evelyn M. Brown]

BAR BOTTLES

In some ways, the United States during the 19th Century was a land of pretense and ostentation. Noting this characteristic, the scholarly Alastair Cooke feels that we were in the throes of a mild inferiority complex. We exhibited marked tendencies toward prettying things up, making mundane things appear grander and sometimes bigger than they really were.

Our ladies piled their hair high on their heads, reduced the diameters of their waists with tightly-laced corsets, and vastly expanded the circumfer-ence of the adjacent portion of their anatomies with huge, imagination-defying bustles. In our architecture, simple log cabins were adorned with massive and misleading multi-faceted false fronts, lending a sense of opulence to their rather austere pioneer surroundings.

Most of America was still agrarian in the 1880's and very little of the goods purchased by the consumer came in any sort of prepared containers. Open bins, barrels, sacks and wooden crates stood in long rows at the front of the grocer's counter. If you wanted liquid products, like vinegar or kerosene (coal oil) for lamps, you brought your own pouring-spout can. A potato plugged the hole. Dried peas, corn and tea were measured and sold by the scoop. The practice of toting a lard pail to the corner saloon for beer was likewise widely

FROM LEFT, a Booz Whiskey, a cod-liver oil "for the morning after," a Great Western Tonic, a Doyle's Hop Bitters, a Warners Safe Kidney and Liver Cure, a White Horse, and a Duffy's Malt Whiskey. [Collection of Evelyn M. Brown]

accepted. Then came a quiet revolution, with broader public acceptance of bottles. And for the saloon trade, some of the most elegant glass containers of all time were produced. Skilled labor was cheap, and there was a genuine sense of pride in personal craftsmanship. Handsomely embossed designs were worked directly into the glass, not just printed on a cheap glue-backed label as is the current practice.

Many of the bottles were moulded into intricate and fanciful shapes by a variety of painstaking processes. In fact, the colloquial term, "booze," came from the embossing on bottles of E. G. Booz's Old Cabin Whiskey. The rare Booz bottles were actually shaped like little cabins. The chimney was the bottle's neck. A cork was put in the neck "to stop the smoke."

Some of the finest examples of the glassmaker's craft were produced from top-quality flint glass.

The product name, a catchy slogan, and sometimes the distiller's or dispenser's name, appeared embossed on the body or the base of the bottle. The Arcade Saloon of Cheyenne, Wyoming, sold Old Crow Whiskey in specially embossed bottles that bore the names of W. A. Gaines & Co., and Phil Kerrigan & Co. The saloon name and the city also appeared in raised letters. A similarly embossed bottle was used by the Charles Kayser Saloon in Telluride, Colorado. Sometimes, the raised letters were enameled or adorned with gilt paint. A few specimen's used primarily for display behind the bar had the lettering etched directly into the glass. Eastern distillers, mostly those of Kentucky, filled beautiful glass containers for their Western customers. The same liquor was bottled in completely different containers for the Eastern trade.

Glass pigmentation of liquor containers was by

FROM RIGHT TO LEFT: A Tiffany Club brandy, a Benedictine miniature and full-size bottle, and a Dominican wine.
[Collection of Evelyn M. Brown]

no means standardized. Many were clear, others bore a slight blue or green coloration. The popular Duffy's Malt Whiskey bottles were dark brown. Honey amber or sun color of one cast or another were also popular, particularly for whiskies. A lesser number of blue, amethyst (or violet), green, olive and amber-red bottles have turned up among collectors in recent years. Many whiskies had applied, or blob, tops and most of them depended on common corks for their closures. Pewter screw-caps and fancy glass-stoppers were not uncommon. Some bar bottles were square, while others assumed the more-common round shape. There were also pinch bottles.

In general, liquor containers can be classified as one of two types. First, the personal or individual ones, usually flasks, and the public bottles, ordinarily, but not always, cylindrical in shape. Long necks were characteristic of a large number of public liquor bottles, particularly the whiskies. But personal flasks had shorter necks, were mostly of clear glass, and, to facilitate their being carried in the pocket, some were made in the familiar coffin-flask shape. Others assumed the round "pumpkin seed" configuration, were relatively flat, and were as common as communicable diseases. They came in several sizes, as do the more conventionally-shaped flasks of today.

FROM RIGHT TO LEFT: A "Celtic Line" bottle used for wine, brandy or whisky; a fish bottle; Warner's Safe bottle; and a Boston square brandy. [Collection of Evelyn M. Brown]

Containers used for champagne or wine were — and some still are — recognizable by their depressions, kick-ups, or push-ups in the bases. Kick-ups were not a means of cheating the consumer on content, but their real purpose may be obscure. Some people are convinced that the kick-up affected effervescence. Others feel that it provided more glass surface and made the bottle stronger. Wine bottles were moulded with long tapering necks. Their tops were finished with a laid-on ring, date line, or applied lip, depending on the period of their manufacture. In color, they were quite varied, but red, amber, blue and green were the most common.

Early ale and stout was bottled in pottery or clay containers. The first imported beers and ales came in pottery bottles. Later, beer and ale bottles, rarely embossed, were primarily of brown or of dark olive-green glass, and some were nearly black. Generally smaller than most of the bottles just described, they held about a pint. Wooden or iron moulds, two and three-piece types, were widely employed and seam marks are clearly visible on these old bottles. Although most of the beer sold over the bar came from heavy oak barrels that were racked horizontally under the bar; some of it was bottled, too. One barrel-head that was found recently bore the words "Green River, Owensboro,

FROM LEFT, a pair of Case Gins, a Dominican wine, the rare Tippecanoe, a Benedictine liqueur and its miniature sample. [Collection of Evelyn M. Brown]

Kentucky. The Whiskey Without A Headache." Eastern barreled-whisky suffered from the interpretations of its Western dispensers who cared little for the reputation of its brand name or their own reputations for honesty. Barrel-delivered whisky was diluted or "stretched" by the addition of water. To cover their deception, a plug of tobacco could be nailed to the inside of the barrel. Iodine was put in some whisky. And then, there was the commercially available product named "Essence of Old Bourbon," sometimes called the "bartender's friend," especially prepared to encourage dishonesty and fatter profits — at the customer's expense.

In an effort to salvage their reputations for integrity, some of the better Kentucky distillers went to heavily embossed bottles that were corked, dated and sealed with lead prior to shipment into the West — hence, the success and popularity of a guaranteed product that was contained in an exclusive type of bottle that was distinctly Western.

Even so, there were people who refilled these bottles with their own brands of Red Eye for sale under the original brand name. Most modern liquor bottles carry the notation that federal law prohibits re-use of these bottles. This is a protection for the producer and supposedly assures that the customer gets what he has paid for. Eastern saloonkeepers were more ethical and got plainer bottles for their pains.

For the occasional saloon customer, who imbibed less often, bartenders kept a limited supply of drugstore tonics, bitters and sarsaparillas. Allegedly, medicinal and sometimes mildly alcoholic, these shrub-root-based concoctions were widely advertised as blood purifiers, aphrodisiacs, as being good for common skin disorders, irregularity and other bowel ailments, kidney, bladder, and liver cures, as a help for poor appetites, "male weaknesses," and for a host of other quasi-medical calamities limited only by the imagination of the bartender and the gullibility of

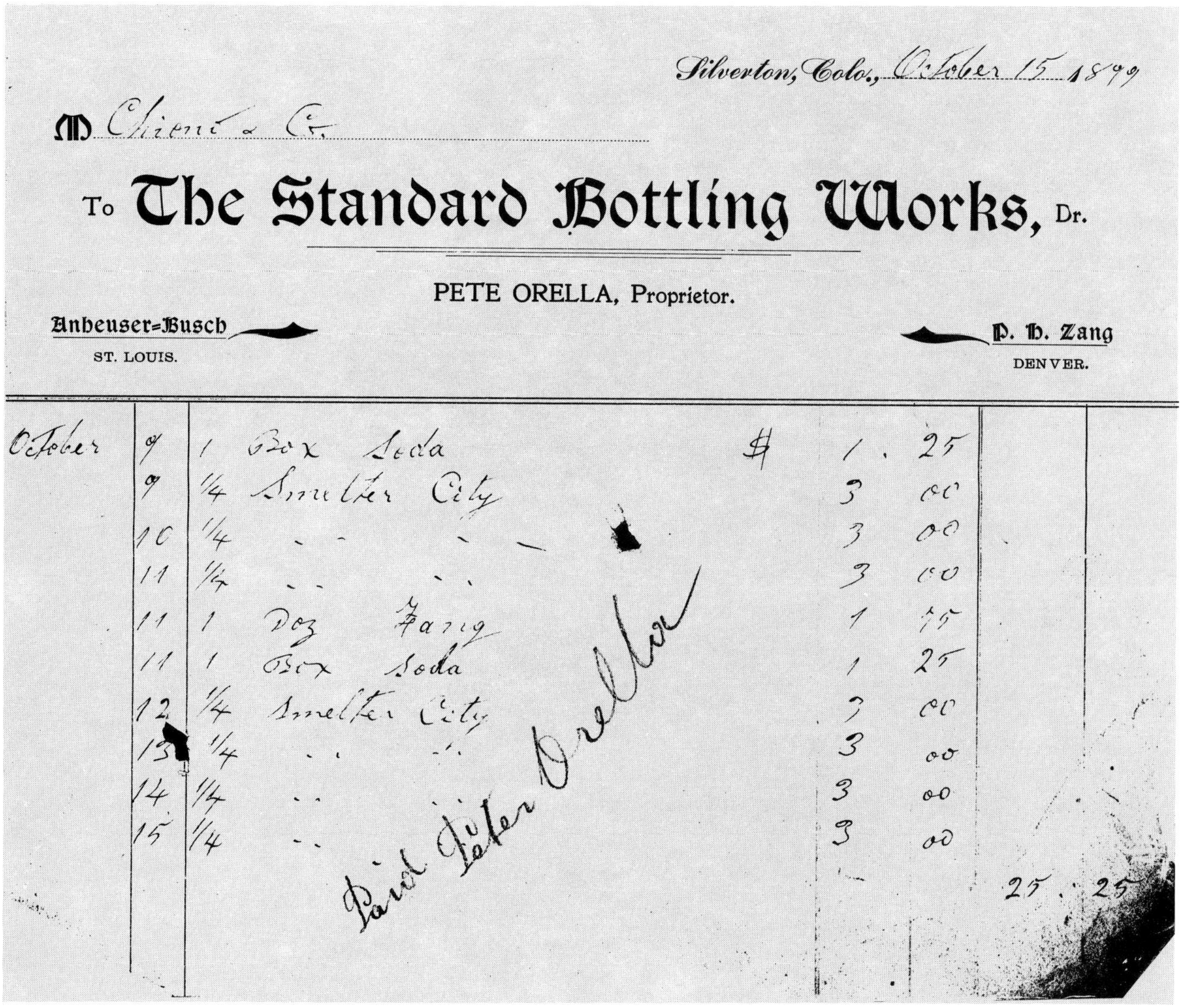

Silverton, Colo., October 15 1879

M Chiori & Co.

To The Standard Bottling Works, Dr.

PETE ORELLA, Proprietor.

Anheuser-Busch — ST. LOUIS.

P. H. Zang — DENVER.

October	9	1 Box Soda	$	1.25
	9	1/4 Smelter City		3 00
	10	1/4 " "		3 00
	11	1/4 " "		3 00
	11	1 Doz Zang		1 75
	11	1 Box Soda		1 25
	12	1/4 Smelter City		3 00
	13	1/4 " "		3 00
	14	1/4 " "		3 00
	15	1/4 " "		3 00
				25.25

Paid Peter Orella

[Collection of Fritz Klinke]

his customer. Most of these potables came in square brown bottles, although some were round, green and nearly all had short necks.

H. H. Warner's Tippecanoe bottle was one of the most unusual of the tonic containers. It was round, tall and embossed to resemble a tree trunk. But its neck was a real conversation piece. It featured a broad, rounded, mushroom or exaggerated flanged top. Its design anticipated the attachment of a rawhide thong so that the bottle could be tied to a saddle.

Brandy bottles followed no particular pattern, but most were heavily embossed. Some, like the Tiffany Club, had bulging "ladies' leg" necks and pumpkin-shaped round-shouldered bodies. Gin bottles also followed few rules. Gordon's London Dry Gin, and its many imitators, came in clear, embossed, square bottles with a slight green or blue tint. The unusual Case Gin bottles were moulded from a sparkling, nearly opaque, textured olive-green glass. Generally square in shape, they taper down from a broad shoulder to a somewhat-smaller base.

For the aesthetically inclined saloon customer, the multi-colored and fancifully shaped array of shiny decanters were an attraction in themselves. They were certainly no less a part of accepted saloon decor than the finely polished, dark mahogany bars, or the eye-level — equally shapely — paintings that adorned the walls of America's 19th Century saloons.

AN EXAMPLE of a Methodist Temperance pledge certificate. [Collection of Barbara Adams]

Chapter 12

IN COMMON WITH MOST REFORM MOVEMENTS, the few had spoiled things for the many. A lesser number of irresponsible persons have caused today's motorists to be burdened with insulting over-regulation, made necessary by a minority of drivers who should not have been licensed in the first place. A similar parallel can be seen in the confusing labyrinth of marriage-and-divorce laws and the havoc that has resulted. And so it was to some extent with the saloon business, where an insensitive minority perpetuated abuses that grew worse with each telling, until the entire industry was assumed to be a monstrous evil.

Very few places banned saloons, but fines were sometimes levied if they became obstreperous. Public drunkennes and excessive drinking were covered by ordinances in most towns, but were difficult rules to enforce. While not all saloons were vice dens, some of them were located in the "entertainment district" of a town, along with red-light houses, billiard halls, gambling halls, dime-a-dance joints, and, at times, next door to opium dens. So, when reformers appeared — usually led by ladies of good repute — guilt by association was presumed, since all presented alluring diversions to their potentially wandering spouses. Admittedly, not every saloon was a family place. Some of them were dreadful dives that should have been put out of business long before the legal axe fell. Carlsbad, New Mexico, was first known as Eddy — however, cowboy carousing gave it a tough reputation. Incensed citizens forced a name change in the interest of a new image. They also decreed that gambling halls, bordellos and saloons must move outside the town limits. The new location was two miles south of the community; and for a time, the whole operation was housed in a huge barn-like adobe building called the "Chihuahua."

V. H. Whitlock, who wrote so entertainingly of cowboy life on the staked plains, described an experience in that institution. When a shooting began in the saloon-and-gambling part of the structure, flying bullets smashed the bar mirror and extinguished the lamps. Dancehall girls screamed in the finest Hollywood tradition. Chairs and gambling tables were overturned and smashed, while poker chips and coins rolled about on the floor. Young Whitlock dropped to the floor and took refuge behind a barrel of whisky. Then came the dull thud of a falling body and the scent of burned gunpowder. Patrons exited through the swinging doors, and some of the more impatient went through the windows. When the unbroken lamps were lit again, the room looked as though an Oklahoma cyclone had passed through it. The dead body was slumped over a whisky barrel and the contents of the barrel were spurting out of a bullet hole. Cause of the shooting was not revealed, if known.

Kansas has long been the most temperance-minded of the Western states. Curiously, it all started in the wild cowboy towns of Dodge City and Abilene — probably as a negative reaction to the raw life styles found on their so-called Texas streets. In 1879, drys in Kansas passed the Murray Law as a constitutional amendment, prohibiting the sale of intoxicants. The people ratified it in the general election of 1880, and it became law in 1881. Temperance forces saw this as a beginning in controlling the end-of-track cattle towns with their wide-open vice districts.

But inadequate enforcement facilities resulted in

Revenue and Taxes

THE STATE PENITENTIARY, CANON CITY, COLORADO.

The COST of Canon City Penitentiary to the State of Colorado for 1909 was $116,000.00. Ninety-five per cent of the prisoners, so Warden Tynan says, are there because of drink. Therefore, $100,200.00 of this amount should be charged to the saloon. Who REALLY PAYS THAT BILL?

The Reformatory at Buena Vista COST for the same period $57,000.00. Allowing that the same per cent were there because of drink, $54,150.00 more can be charged to the saloon.

A good authority estimates that 90 per cent of the inmates of the State Home for Dependent Children, are there because of drink. Another item to be charged to the saloon.

FIGURES FROM RECORD OF CLERK OF DENVER COUNTY FOR 1909.

Per cents show the estimated expense caused by the saloon. This statement was prepared by Halsted L. Ritter.

Juvenile Court	$ 12,316.89	50%	$ 6,158.45
Justice of the Peace Courts	19,958.72	50%	9,979.36
Police Court	4,600.00	50%	2,300.00
Fifth Division District Court	15,000.00	75%	11,250.00	$ 29,681.81
Support of Poor	42,370.40	50%	21,185.50
Poor Farm	30,118.50	25%	7,529.25
County Hospital	79,532.71	25%	19,886.25	48,601.00
County Jail	47,898.58	75%	35,923.95
City Jail and Police Department	265,000.00	50%	132,500.00
District Attorney	32,775.00	60%	19,665.00
Assistant City Attorney	1,800.00	50%	900.00
Sheriff	23,785.33	60%	14,271.20	203,260.15
Keeley Institute	189.00	....	189.00
Gatlin Institute	1,300.00	....	1,300.00	1,489.00
	$576,294.24		$283,938.06
License for 467 saloons			280,200.00

TWO PIECES of anti-saloon literature from Colorado's Church Federation Against the Saloon. [Collection of Jim Wright]

the creation of new evils in place of those the law sought to eliminate. Graft and special privilege were rampant. Saloons were put out of business in the rurally oriented eastern counties; but in the plains cattle country, personal freedom was cherished jealously, and the Murray amendment proved unenforceable. Sodbusters had taken up homesteads in what had been cattle country and became numerous enough to impose their Calvinist ideals. They associated all of the assorted evils of gambling, prostitution, shootings and general uproar with saloons. Besides, they had plenty to drink on their own farms.

Saloon-men were arrested in the inevitable raids, but the swinging doors continued to swing. Enos

Blair, saloon-hating editor of the Caldwell, Kansas, *Free Press* bitterly attacked the saloons. He refused to heed warnings to soft pedal his tirades, and his home was put to the torch. His presses were demolished; and he fled the town. Riotous intoxication and fierce patriotism got all mixed up. Floating saloons poled their way up and down the Kaw and Kansas rivers. Frustrated enforcement men were thrown overboard, while imbibers rejoiced tumultuously.

Noisy hymn singing and mass prayers beyond the swinging doors, tactics dear to Eastern-establishment lady prohibitionists, were first used to annoy the thirsty of Topeka, Lecompton and Lawrence in 1880. Names of those who frequented the thirst parlors were written down by lady bar-watchers. Men with black pork-pie hats joined the ladies on parades through the streets. Brass bands — when available — tootled the message of salvation through abstinence from strong drink.

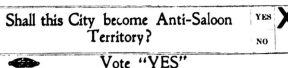

Somehow, it all seemed to work. On March 10, 1881, Kansas officially went dry. Almost immediately thereafter the first speakeasy began sliding the secret panel in its door in Manhattan, and equipment for making bathtub gin was hastily installed in college dormitories all across the state. Americans heard about the paradox of Kansas prohibition from stand-up comedians who chortled their way through tiresome one-liners about how "Kansas staggered to the polls to vote dry." Twentieth-Century Americans have heard on their radios how airplanes closed their bars while flying over Kansas.

As early as 1852, the Sons of Temperance were at work in California's Mother Lode Country; and reformed hardrock-men had forsaken their liquid ego-fortifiers and had taken to water. Some repeated a free-swinging adaptation of *Hamlet*, entitled *The Toper's Soliloquy*. "To drink or not to drink, that is the question; whether 'tis nobler in the mind, etc. . . . ''

In early-day Denver, most of the saloons were found along Blake Street. William Newton Byers, founder and editor of Colorado's oldest daily newspaper, the *Rocky Mountain News*, was the source of most of the opposition to the saloons. A favorite tactic of saloonkeepers involved recruiting whole battalions of drunks to be marched past the *News* office, while being as noisy and obstreperous as possible. For a long time, Byers chose to be armed while working. Denver was a wide-open town for saloons and for advocates of a Sunday-closing law as well. The *Rocky Mountain News* joined with the supporters of a "blue law." Curiously, help came from a quite-unexpected quarter — the local bartenders, who figured it might be nice to have a day off once in a while.

Early in the present century, the Women's Christian Temperance Union (WCTU) promoted a demonstration in Deadwood, which provoked such a furor that a law was passed forcing saloons to remove curtains from their windows. Most men completely missed the point, feeling that WCTU actions were prompted by a curiosity about what went on behind the swinging doors. And after passage of the curtainless covenant, women could not even cross the street to avoid passing a saloon, because more often than not, a like-establishment reposed on the other side of the thoroughfare. It also was without curtains.

Temperance-minded ladies thought of the saloons as sources of disease, and many insisted that their husbands strip and put on clean clothing from the skin out when they got home at night from the saloon.

Even those who ordinarily abstained from alco-

EVADING THE LIQUOR LAW in Colorado Springs. From ''Leslie's Weekley'' of 1877. [Western History Collection —Denver Public Library]

holic pursuits were subjected to their influence at Rhyolite, Nevada. All of the water for the town's use had to be hauled-in from Beatty; and the containers used were whisky barrels, which had just been emptied. This whisky-stained water was sold to residents for $2 to $5 a barrel. Temperance persons protested loudly.

Many persons sought to bring about reforms where public drunkenness had been a problem. Like the saloons they opposed, there was no shortage of reformers. But coins usually have two faces. There is a delicious tale that Carry Nation once became quite fond of Dr. David Hostetter's Stomach Bitters. She almost gave it a testimonial. Then she found out that the stuff contained 47 percent alcohol and the deal was off. For a time, the most militant opposition to saloons was led by Miss Frances E. Willard, who became president of the Women's Christian Temperance Union. She hoped to use the votes of women to outlaw saloons.

HERE ARE TWO rare temperance items: A pledge and an
inscribed mug. Both are from the Methodist Band of Hope.
[Collection of Edith Ritchie]

Miss Willard opposed alcohol, the lack of equality for women in sex, and traditional-institutionalized Christianity. She was troubled because some churches required that women cover their heads while worshiping, while men were not bound by any such rule.

Frances Willard schemed to have temperance viewpoints included in school books to assure that the next generation would grow up in horror of liquor and its effects. Some of her inserts suggested that drinking parents handed down poisoning, mental retardation and insanity to their offspring.

One example suggested that the alcohol-sodden person might become so saturated that accidental incineration could take place.

Miss Willard started out to preach in all of the bigger towns across the country, using the census of 1870. By 1883, she had visited all of them, except a couple of state capitals. The city fathers of Lewiston, Idaho, heard that she was on the way and quarantined the town in the name of a diphtheria epidemic. Frances Willard tried working within the system through the established political parties. She tried the Democrats first, but without tangible results. In 1884, the Republican Convention gave her a 15-minute hearing while a brewers' committee got an entire hour from William McKinley. She finally joined the Prohibition party. However, compared with the obstreperous and unpredictable Carry Nation, Frances Willard's anti-saloon activities were mild.

Carry Nation — sometimes misspelled as Carrie — did the Lord's work with a dollar axe, smashing glassware and defacing paintings of scantily clad nymphs and satyrs in the liquor-dispensing strongholds of sin. Carry had an unfortunate childhood, and many unfortunate things about her mother's mental state have been printed. Insanity, of course, is not hereditary, but its invironmental effects are something else again.

To compound the "felony," Carry had two unhappy exposures to matrimony. Her first husband was a dedicated rumpot of heroic capacity. He died in delirium tremens. Carry lost little time in mourning. She married again almost at once. It was in 1877 that she met and married her second spouse, a 50-year-old widower, Rev. David Nation. She was 31 at the time. The relationship was an unhappy one for both persons, ending in a divorce in 1901. Rev. Nation brought the action and was awarded the divorce because of his wife's reputation with an axe in saloons.

Carry joined the Women's Christian Temperance Union in Medicine Lodge, Kansas, in 1895. She had but one answer to all her problems. She blamed liquor for her feeble-minded relatives, her insane daughter and the failure of both her matrimonial excursions. But she did have a few other curious hates, too. Among them were the "filthy rags of fashion," judges, female ankles and bosoms, short and long skirts, cigar smokers, William McKinley and Theodore Roosevelt, the Republican and Democratic parties, love-making in public, and corsets.

At age 54, Mrs. Nation first used violence on a thirst parlor. The place was Medicine Lodge, Kansas, and the saloon belonged to Martin Strong. Allegedly, Carry led 200 women and children on the march. They set up an organ in the street outside and sang hymns. Strong's customers hummed the tunes and swung their beer mugs in time with the music. Armed only with an umbrella, Carry Nation entered the saloon. When she began to harangue him, Strong physically put her back outside onto the board-sidewalk. However, before she departed, Carry had brought about the closing of seven saloons in Medicine Lodge.

On June 6, 1900, Carry Nation entered Kiowa, Kansas, and destroyed three saloons. Rocks, brickbats and an old iron, wrapped in newspapers, were her weapons. But before long, she discovered the dollar axe that would become her trademark for years to come. Apparently, she first employed the axe in James Burnes' saloon on Douglas Avenue in Wichita, Kansas. At Topeka, the pro-saloon contingent hired huge negro ex-slaves as guards when they heard that Carry and the WCTU were on the way to their community. Allegedly, the ex-slaves were armed with bludgeons, clubs and sawed-off shotguns.

A somewhat more original and less-dangerous ploy was used by Antonio Romani. He installed a

TEMPERANCE GROUPS circulated tokens like these to inspire anti-saloon sentiment. [Collection of Robert L. Brown]

DENVER'S WCTU MISSION. Note the resemblance of lady at right to Carry Nation. Western History Collection —Denver Public Library.]

A "WOMAN'S RIGHTS" SALOON envisioned by the "Denver Times," July 5, 1901, after an "equal rights" decision by Judge Peter L. Palmer. [Western History Collection—Denver Public Library]

WHEN THE WOMEN ACT ON JUDGE PALMER'S DECISION.

This is what we can expect in the nature of a woman's rights saloon.

cage of rats in the middle of the floor of his saloon. A guard was instructed to open the cage if a WCTU smasher tried to enter. The "white ribboners" heard about it and gave Romani's a wide berth. A few saloonkeepers sent axes to Carry as gifts; some were double-bitted. A counter-attack on Carry Nation was launched by the wives, mothers and sisters of saloonkeepers. They fought a street battle outside John Schilling's bar in Enterprise, Kansas. There probably were no winners — at least no victory was ever announced in print. In February of 1901, Carry Nation's forces reduced Topeka to a state of seige for days. Her crusaders smashed saloons and provoked street fights.

Another successful defense tactic was employed Nation entered his place, he rushed to her, grasped her hand, claimed that he was converted and asked her to kneel and pray with him. Following a prolonged period of invocation, she left without even unsheathing her axe. Needless to say, the place was back in full swing as soon as Carry was beyond the city limits.

Mrs. Nation once accused Theodore Roosevelt of operating a private saloon in his railroad car during a campaign swing through Kansas. Kansas was dry then, and Mrs. Nation suggested that T.R. should have been arrested like any other dive-keeper. After he had become President, Teddy twice denied Carry an audience at the White House.

During her destructive crusades, Mrs. Nation invariably took pleasure in pulverizing any voluptuous paintings that hung inside the barroom under attack. One saloon displayed a placard that said, "All Nations Welcome Except Carry." She once vandalized a barroom nude with her axe while insisting that it "hung in a place where it was not even decent for a woman to frequent when she had her clothes on."

There actually were Carry Nation Bars in Leavenworth, Kansas, and in St. Louis. Several drinks that really packed a whallop were also named for her. When saloon-men along Cripple Creek's Bennett and Myers avenues heard that Mrs. Nation was on the train from Colorado Springs, headed for their town, they took up a hasty collection. A nestegg of nearly $5,000 was sent to her when the train pulled in. The offer was conditional on her just staying in the train. Local legend insists that she took it and that is how Cripple Creek escaped her axe.

Butte, Montana, was the scene of Mrs. Nation's final saloon smashing. January 6, 1910, was the date. Supposedly, there was hand-to-hand combat between Carry and May Maloy, the saloon pro-

CARRY NATION'S MAGAZINE, "The Smasher's Mail," showed Carry. (Note misspelling on the cover.) [Western History Collection—Denver Public Library]

prietress. When Carry began ripping down the saloon art and smashing the bottled stock, May jumped her and the donnybrook was on. Mrs. Maloy was the more-able pugilist and Carry departed a badly beaten woman. In one version of the encounter, she retired to the Arkansas hills to die. However, the date of her death was July 2, 1911, over a year after her scrap with Mrs. Maloy.

Between Frances Williard and Carry Nation, the saloon business was kept in a state of unrest for about three decades. But the saloon business just went rolling along anyway.

PROHIBITION, BOOTLEGGERS AND SPEAKEASIES

Prohibition was a national hassle between the drys and the wets. Before it was over, neighbor had been turned against neighbor, pastors were alienated from thirsty parishioners, and Al Smith, a worthy but "wet" candidate, was denied the Presidency. England's King George V was furious that an American state would presume to meddle in so personal a right as man's appetite for spirits. He cut short his state visit and dashed off to Canada where a person could have his draught without interference.

America's prohibition movement had begun somewhere back in the middle decades of the 19th Century. Much of the support for national prohibition came from the middle class, agriculturally oriented small towns of middle America. It was in Maine where the first "dry law" was passed, and the date was 1851. Clergymen and abstainers worked together in the belief that people needed to be protected against forces that undermined their self-control.

Anti-saloon clubs were formed and did a hatchet job on saloons. Bacchanalian tales of moral wrongdoing behind the swinging doors were invented and widely circulated, growing more lurid with each exciting rendition. And those same anti-saloon forces usually described all killings as "whisky murders," just as a matter of course.

Businessmen promptly jumped on the bandwagon when it was pointed out to them that absenteeism, abandoned families, reduced efficiency in their plants — and, therefore, profits — and illness might in part be traced to chronic intoxication. Public almshouses, jails, drunk tanks and asylums also increased the deplorable tax burden. Then — even as now — America treated the effect rather than the cause and charged off to joust with the windmills by ending the sale of alcoholic beverages.

The Women's Christian Temperance Union was formed in 1874. It was an organized effort to bring Protestant churches into the battle. A more-effective movement was spawned in 1893, when Methodist, Baptist, Congregational and Presbyterian church representatives met in Oberlin, Ohio, and formed the Anti-Saloon League. Their vigorous efforts resulted in passage of local-option laws which permitted counties to adopt prohibition. They also advocated passage of the Webb-Kenyon Interstate Liquor Act, which outlawed transporting liquor in "dry" states.

Then came the Eighteenth Amendment to the U.S. Constitution, passed in January of 1919, the high-water mark of Anti-Saloon League achievement. This, of course, prohibited the transport, sale or manufacture of intoxicants. Only Connecticut and Rhode Island failed to adopt the Eighteenth, or Prohibition, Amendment. Mississippi was the first of the states to ratify it on January 8, 1918. When Nebraska followed suit on January 16, 1919, the required 36th state had provided approval and the law became effective on January 16, 1920.

So, America adopted the Eighteenth Amendment and went dry by constitutional edict. In almost no time, the bootleggers had fired up their "alky" cookers and had started "getting the mash ready for the cookers." The term bootlegger was adapted from the West to the southern hills of Georgia and Tennessee, where illegal still operators carried their products to customers in the loose-fitting tops of their boots. This practice avoided payment of federal taxes on distilled spirits.

Prohibition changed many aspects of public and private morality. Men and women began drinking together and getting drunk in the name of togetherness. Whether or not this has contributed to the increase in juvenile delinquency makes for an interesting argument. And who can resist considering the enormous increase in adult crime in this same post-saloon era? The arguments, of course, are hypothetical on both sides.

However, vice and crime did not disappear with the closing of saloons. The Volstead Act had to be written to enforce the Eighteenth Amendment's provisions by defining the alcoholic content of intoxicants. Congress passed the Volstead Act in October of 1919. Woodrow Wilson vetoed it and Congress passed it over his veto on January 17, 1920. It remained in effect until passage of the Twenty-First (Repeal) Amendment.

Enforcement of the Volstead restrictions was impossible. By the middle of the next decade, this era had become known as the Roaring Twenties. Smuggling, speakeasies, "blind pigs" and rum-running on the high seas had become rampant. Drinking associations, ironically called Volstead Clubs, flourished. Illegal stills were everywhere and bathtub gin became a household word. Police officials who tried to enforce the Volstead Act were referred to in some cities as "hooch hounds." It has been estimated that sympathetic physicians wrote more than 11-million prescriptions annually covering alcoholic preparations "for medicinal purposes."

The Volstead Act created a new profession for thousands of Americans — that of bootlegger. This

THIS WIDE-ANGLE VIEW shows the interior of the restored saloon at the South Park City museum display in Fairplay, Colorado. [Collection of Robert L. Brown]

profession required no scholastic education nor academic sanction. Federal courts were choked with liquor cases, while other decisions waited their turn. By June 17, 1920, the district attorney of Chicago reported a backlog of 568 cases. The resulting struggle has been a never-ending source of material for motion pictures, mystery stories and the old bromides of television.

On February 28, 1921, two carloads of patent medicine containing 55-percent alcohol were seized by government inspectors in Chicago. On June 6, 1920, the special train of the Massachusetts delegation to the Republican National Convention was raided by prohibition agents who seized half its stock of liquor.

William Jennings Bryan, far-famed as the "barefoot-boy orator of the Platte," was defeated three times as the Democratic Presidential candidate. Bryan, a militant teetotaler, became a champion of the religiously oriented prohibition forces. But Bryan got his jollies in other ways. A dedicated glutton, he literally ate himself to death;

and no one proposed restrictive laws to punish the stores that sold him the candy and other sweets that helped put this fine man into his grave.

In any case, virtually all of the efforts of these well-intentioned reformers came to naught. Certainly, prohibition did not accomplish what its advocates had predicted, although there was probably less drinking than before. "Drys" salvaged what they could from the "noble experiment" by claiming that the boost in savings-bank deposits and our nation's remarkable prosperity, had come about as a result of the closing of saloons. "Wets" insisted that crime had been fostered and that there had been a greatly increased disrespect for the law.

Actually, it had become profitable to violate the liquor laws. Rum-running became the basis of more than one large fortune. Al Capone of Cook County, Illinois, controlled the availability of illegal home brew in the estimated 10,000 "speak-easies" that operated in Chicago and Cicero. In the decade prior to 1930, there were some 500

AT NEVADA CITY, MONTANA, this restored saloon has both swinging and regular doors. [Collection of Robert L. Brown]

gangland murders in that city. Bootlegging and its control and distribution monopoly seem to have been largely responsible for increases in violence in many American cities.

William Rutledge, Detroit's police superintendent at the time, said that 1,500 saloons flourished in that city when prohibition went into effect. Afterwards, he estimated that 15,000 additional illegal sources of liquor existed in Detroit. Extortion and lower-echelon bribery existed. The national incidence of both bombings and murder increased during prohibition.

During prohibition, Detroit was reputed to have had 20,000 "blind pigs," a low-grade speakeasy that sold a very poor quality of moonshine liquor. Many were run by women who doubled as "entertainers" when the price was right. Most "blind pigs" were shoddy and were furnished with temporary fixtures. Bartenders were paid $75 weekly, with $50 bonuses if they were arrested in a raid. If a weekend stay in jail resulted, the bonus was $75. Although some liquor was made locally, much of it was made in Canada and smuggled across the conveniently nearby border.

In the Detroit business district, all sorts of storefront disguises were used to hide the existence of "blind pigs." One was a well-equipped clothing store with specially equipped fitting-rooms in the back where fiery liquids were dispensed. Another "front" had a completely equipped barroom with easy chairs and a white-coated bartender. A luggage shop and a laundry were similarly equipped. Allegedly, there was even an undertaking parlor where liquor-storage vats were concealed in two caskets.

Local wags had a field day with stories that capitalized on the more macabre aspects of booze-juggling in this undertaking establishment. One of these described an elderly man who partook too generously and became violently ill. Soon, the proprietor's hand was seen resting gently on the old man's shoulder as he inquired, "Hardly worth going home, is it?"

By 1927, deaths from alcoholism had increased by 150 percent in the United States. There was a 60 percent increase in "dry" Kansas and a 23 percent increase in "wet" Ohio. Only staid, stable Vermont showed no increase. Deaths were 15 times higher here in the U.S. than in England, which still had saloons.

During prohibition, the ladies of the Women's Christian Temperance Union succeeded in associating liquor with the negative aspects of our whole middle-class Judeo-Christian tradition of public and private morality. Their answer to drinking problems would eliminate the sources of booze, completely disregarding the fact that when one avenue of personal frustration is closed, the same frustration will seek a new outlet. The social conditions that make a person misuse alcohol do not vanish with the alcohol. Hence, the unacceptable outlet may become wife-beating, exhibitionist automobile driving, the use of narcotics, or heaven knows what other horrors.

After Franklin Delano Roosevelt's election and passage of the Twenty-First Amendment in 1932, some efforts were made to revive the saloon, but too much had changed. Life now progressed at a much more accelerated pace. Women openly expected to be admitted to drinking places. Too many cooks had burned too many beans and it just did not seem the same any more. Newer names had to be invented to describe places where alcoholic solace could be purchased. After the Twenty-First Amendment repealed the ill-starred Eighteenth, even the word "saloon" had become so associated with evil in the public mind that the negative connotation still survives today.

For over a half century now, a majority of our American states have had no saloons. But the name survives in a few Western states. Commercialized recreation, packaged liquor stores, movies (including the biologically oriented outdoor "drive-ins"), bowling alleys and the automobile have replaced the socializing influences of the saloon. More than half of our proposals of marriage now occur in cars, and liquor has become a statistically measurable factor in a majority of America's automobile accidents. Only four percent of America's drivers drink, but they account for 57 percent of our accidents.

Since we now have drive-in banks, restaurants, laundries, hotels, whole vacation homes mounted on wheels, and the recent popularity of drive-in churches, perhaps a drive-in saloon with "honky-tonk" girls darting about on motor-scooters might prove popular! Assuredly, some of the side effects would be avidly studied by our sociologists during the next few years. Technology, perhaps more than any other factor, was the thing that killed the oldtime saloon.

During prohibition, and for a number of years thereafter, certain brewers and distributors embarked upon a public-relations program designed to curry public favor. At state fairs, customers would be treated to a dose of the nostalgia of a bygone era. Enormous and brightly painted beer-delivery wagons would come rumbling onto county racetracks between sulky racing contests.

A great fuss was made over the immaculately curried teams of huge Clydesdale draft horses, one of the few animals strong enough to pull such loads. Using six to eight horses per wagon, the sound and vibration of massive, pounding hoofs shook the grandstands and produced a thunderous rumble that was most impressive to the local Hirams. The stark contrast between Clydesdales and common little race-horses never failed to amaze rural spectators in traditionally dry middle America.

Sometimes spirited contests were staged between opposing teams, with the skillful drivers backing, wheeling and pirouetting their ponderous equines intricately between alley-like obstacles as they lined-up wagon tailgates against imaginary saloon loading platforms. Big loading mats of braided rope were spread out with an almost religious ceremony to cushion the beer barrels as they were rolled from the wagons.

As a ritualistic finale, the burly drivers pounded wooden spigots or bungstarters into the barrels, a customary courtesy rendered to bartenders by thoughtful distributors. Then, they galloped the teams around the track again, shaking the whole place a second time before exiting. Judging by the profusion of ornate rings that adorned the harnesses, the brewers almost singlehandedly supported the celluloid business in America at the same time.

In 1969, Internal Revenue Service records showed that taxes were paid on 985,681 gallons of whisky, gin, vodka and other distilled spirits. In Washington, D.C., the Distilled Spirits Institute tells us that the legal drinking age in America is now 21, except for New York and Louisiana where it is legal at 18. A number of other states allow beer drinking at 18 or 20. In the West, these include Idaho, Colorado, Kansas and Oklahoma.

Reformers started early, did their work effectively, and are still active. As early as 1910, Curtis Publications had banned most liquor advertising and refused to allow pictures of steins or wine glasses. The rule for the *Ladies Home Journal* said, "No reference to alcoholic beverages is allowable, and references to wine glasses or steins may not be used." In 1946, the *Woman's Home Companion* set up a similar rule. *The Reader's Digest* has long embraced a like policy for both liquor and tobacco.

Some states, like Colorado, passed laws so that no business could use even the word "saloon." Prohibition against drinking while standing up (people might fall) were written into some county and state statutes. However, public drinking did not stop, even though the rules that governed its protocol had been altered. America's last real saloons closed their doors on January 20, 1920.

THE GRAND IMPERIAL HOTEL BAR in Silverton, Colorado provided the setting for this re-enactment of saloon life. Those posing in this scene were John Shufelt and Vicky Gurule of Sundance Publications, and Mike Mikalis, owner of the hotel. [Photo by Dell A. McCoy]

Chapter 13

THE SALOON TODAY

IF YOU HAPPEN TO BE THE SORT of reader who becomes involved with a subject, you may be just curious enough to wonder about seeing a saloon with "oldtime" atmosphere today. Although the majority of public drinking houses now require that you sit down to imbibe, there are yet some places where a degree of the original atmosphere remains. A number of the surviving old bistros still have the brass rails bolted to the floors, but single-pedestal stools now stand in neat rows along the front of the bar. Today's consumer faces his bartender with both feet on the brass rail, just to keep matters within the law. A lesser number of places have even kept their old brass spittoons, but demonstrations of expectorial marksmanship are discouraged.

In our ghost towns the original buildings are disappearing fast, due in part to vandalism, nearly a century of disuse and the natural attrition of high-altitude weather. Those selected for description within these pages may conceivably be gone by the time you read this.

Manifestly, America's public drinking houses ran the gamut from Colonial taverns through trail saloons, crude-tent establishments and the like, to the final home-away-from-home for the weary frontiersman or miner who sought a brief respite from the monotony of digging gold or herding cattle. It follows, too, that there never was a typical saloon that could pass for a stereotype. Rather, saloons were of many types, not necessarily contiguous in place or time. No two were precisely the same. The peculiar physical environment of the West, distances from other places, and the special attitudes of early populations, all imparted a sense of local color and variety. If any one saloon characteristic stood out in common, it was this very lack of uniformity.

Today, most of the old saloons can be seen only as we view certain other historical entities, as silent, dusty places that, in their own distinctive way, recall a colorful if transitory society to which a substantial part of our Far West owes its beginning, its evolution and its uniqueness.

INDEX